GOING ZERO

Kate Hughes

First published by Canbury Press 2022
This edition published 2022

Canbury Press
Kingston upon Thames, Surrey, United Kingdom
www.canburypress.com

Printed and bound in Great Britain
by Short Run Press in Devon using 100% recycled paper
Revive paper (www.revivepaper.com)
Typeset in Interface and Minion Pro
Cover: Alice Marwick

This is a work of non-fiction

ISBN
Paperback: 978-1-912454-69-3
Ebook: 978-1-912454-66-2

GOING ZERO

Kate Hughes

Canbury

For DJB

CONTENTS

1. The Eye Opener

One afternoon in our small garden I step off the kids' trampoline onto a large outdoor beanbag. It's a brief attempt at fun mum.

But it causes a deep split. The once sturdy canvas, by then sun-bleached and weakened, gives way with a satisfying rip and my foot goes straight through the middle. For a moment, while the family giggle helpfully, the tiny polystyrene balls swirl and eddy around my leg.

In the back of my mind I know why the balls make this beanbag comfortable, fun to own, cheap and easy to buy. It's there to brighten up a neglected patio, but I have otherwise given it little thought.

I'm surprised, though, that *nobody* has given a thought to it bursting – that this beanbag doesn't have an inner lining to stop the balls flying away the second I yank my limb out.

But it doesn't. Within seconds, thousands of white spheres land on the grass. In the lightest of breezes they start to whisper and whirl around, settling on plants, pots, the children's hair, clothes, before scuttling across the gravel. I dive towards the back door to get something to start collecting them all up but by the time I turn around the scene is a blizzard. Our daughter, who is three, has started 'swimming' enthusiastically, hooting with delight as she hurls armfuls of plastic snow high in the air. You can picture the scene.

My husband David and I begin clearing up. We coax our daughter away from the best sensory play session ever and march in with dustpans, buckets and brushes. By now, I can see the polystyrene floating into the corners of the garden, over the wall, slipping into the drain. It's 98% air – I can't contain it.

In the end, I spend six hours outside with the hoover, emptying tiny pearly white balls over and over again into our black wheelie bin even as thousands escape. Even with the lid on tight, I know the moment the bin is tipped into the refuse lorry and carted away, those balls will be released into a bleak landfill site – and the pollution I am directly responsible for will start again.

I feel sick at the pit of my stomach. A series of commercial pressures and events – from our demand for an affordable but unimportant item, to its delivery, storage and treatment – has resulted in us fundamentally polluting not only our own backyard, but also the world's water system. Forever. In a few seconds.

Years later, you can lift any piece of gravel by the side of our house and still find polystyrene balls. They will probably be there for thousands of years, because we just didn't think.

Polystyrene is such a common material that we don't register it anymore. It's used in everything from surfboards to takeaway containers and car parts, but we know it best in the form of the rigid puffed packaging.

Polystyrene's makers say it as environmentally friendly, because it helps prevent items being damaged or spoiled, reducing the flow of electrical goods or food heading for landfill. Without doubt, its lightness lowers fuel consumption during transport. It is also techni-

Breaking up with polystyrene

Manufacturers love polystyrene – technically, expanded Polystyrene or EPS. And you can see why. It is inert, feather-light, cheap, a great insulator and can be made with less water and energy than other packaging materials.

But it is also very long-lasting and that's where the problem lies. Though polystyrene blocks often crumble in your hands, the material doesn't actually biodegrade[23] – probably ever. If it is left in the open and exposed to sunlight, it turns to microplastic dust in a few years. If it is buried in landfill, it remains for up to a million years, according to some estimates.

The situation is worse in the oceans. EPS is one of the most common materials found on shorelines and beaches all over the world. You can find it in vast quantities, on the surface of the open ocean and on the seafloor[24], through the water column and in sediment across the globe. The scientific community has been aware that EPS degrades in seawater since the 1970s. The resulting tiny micro or even nano-plastic pieces are commonly ingested by marine animals that mistake it for food[25], simultaneously taking up space in their digestive systems and depriving them of nutrition from other sources.

The jury is still out on the full effects of microplastics such as these styrene monomers higher up the food chain, including on fish- and shellfish-eating humans. The environmental impact of polystyrene, particularly when it disintegrates in water, has prompted nations around the world to introduce complete or partial bans on its manufacture and use. For instance, the EU has banned EPS from takeaway containers and coffee cups.[26]

Sadly, though, its legacy will be with us forever.

cally recyclable, though that seems impossible. As a householder looking to re-house a small amount, I have tried and failed to find anywhere that recycles polystyrene within 50 miles of our home.

And this is the bind we are all in. Environmental scientists talk about a new geological age, one whose strata will be layer upon layer of compressed plastic in myriad forms. Thousands of years from now this is what will represent us. Not the cultural accomplishments, the technological or medical advances, or how we can see billions of light years into space. But plastic.

So these tiny plastic balls are the legacy we've left to our little garden, its soil, the surrounding patchwork of carefully tended gardens, and the neighbourhood water system.

When we finally give up trying to sweep, hoover or at least contain them all, we do what any self-respecting adult does after some long, hot work outdoors – we hit the fridge.

That isn't a life-affirming eco moment either. Every single item of food in there is cocooned in plastic, from last night's Chinese and the slightly slimy bag of salad to the brightly coloured children's plate still hopefully offering leftovers.

I am already uncomfortable about that plate – and not just because the spag bol on it has already been rejected twice.

❀ ❀ ❀

I become aware of how much I, we, have changed without even noticing. I had thought of myself as an environmentalist, and I could luxuriate in the credentials. I had been vegetarian since the age of eight. As a child, I had written to 'the government' demanding action following the *Sea Empress* oil tanker disaster that devastated the Pembrokeshire coast in the 1990s. From my teens I wouldn't join friends in McDonalds on account of its historical links to the clearance of rainforest for cattle grazing.[1]

As a younger adult I had recycled fervently. We'd once carted a bag of recycling across international borders so it wouldn't go to landfill. And, of course, I'd had those endless worthy conversations over too much red wine about whaling or the environmental impact of global manufacturing.

But, really, I was kidding myself about how much I was actually, practically doing to help – because it was very little. As an ordinary family living in an English town, we had become sucked into the intellectual impotence of modern life – an expensive, unhealthy way of consuming and an environmental disaster that threatens our very existence.

There had been a twitch, a pang, a week before Beanbag Day. While grappling with a newborn son, I had stumbled across an article about Bisphenol A or BPA. BPA is used to make plastics for a huge variety of items. Food packaging, the inner coating on cans and jar caps, dental equipment, children's toys and baby items... it's everywhere. Generally, plastics don't react with things around them – it's a key reason for their durability – but BPA can leach into food and liquid, particularly when heated.[2]

Even if you don't heat food, use a plastic container, or drink water that has been in a plastic bottle for a long time, it's difficult to avoid BPA. The human body ingests it, inhales it and absorbs it through the skin and once in the body it can disrupt the endocrine system. This is the collection of glands that use hormones to help regulate the human body. Which means BPA is linked to disorders including fertility, foetal development, the early onset of puberty, brain disorders and hormone-dependent tumours like breast and prostate cancer, to name but a few nasties. And it is found in the urine of 90% of us.[3] The European Union banned BPA from the production of baby bottles back in 2011. But it is still found widely in other items that come into our home, including food packaging.[4] Needless to say, I instantly stopped using clingfilm and bought an expensive glass baby bottle for my tiny son to replace the hand-me-down bottles, cutlery, 'sippy cups' and plates I'd once been so smug about filling our cupboards with for free.[5]

Beanbag Day, though, was the tipping point that finally shook us out of our slumber. So we changed our lifestyle. We changed it that day and we changed it permanently. We started with a complete ban on plastics.

In the past four years, we have rolled out environmentally responsible change across the rest of our lives, from switching our energy supplier to ditching disposable nappies.

Some steps have been hurried and huge, some slow and small. Altogether, our lives are almost unrecognisable from what they were before. We don't own a bin. We don't shop in supermarkets. I haven't been into a petrol station or airport for years.

But there have also been other changes we could not have predicted at the time: how our attitudes to possessions and ownership, nutrition and health, financial priorities and even to personal success would change dramatically, too.

Sometimes, pursuing this lifestyle was lonely, and sometimes it was awkward. But we felt the tide of history swishing in our direction. Six months after Beanbag Day, the UK's TV audience would watch, horrified, as the sinister ghost of a plastic bag slid down the flank of a baby pilot whale on the BBC's *Blue Planet* series. It gave the nation an immediate, irrefutable glimpse of the scale and depth of the impact of our consumption. Plastic would never be seen in the same way again.

More widely, environmental awareness has gone mainstream. We have all been told we need to change our habits if we have a hope of 'saving the world.' The only problem is that nobody has told us what that means. Sure there are siloed discussions around plastic, and meat, and flying, but what does the whole picture look like? What exactly do we need to know – and how and what do we need to change?

✻ ✻ ✻

In the beginning, the biggest problem was the mass of information and misinformation that can quickly engulf you like an avalanche.

It was quite a task trying to pick our way through the production methods behind just one item in an ocean of possessions, bouncing between the most emotive of social media posts and the densest of scientific papers. It felt thankless at best, utterly pointless at worst.

But we have gradually learned to take one aspect of life at a time, over time, usually following the order of rooms in our home or events and activities in our lives to give us some sort of structure and plan.

We break down the habits and assumptions about the products we buy and the facilities and services we use. We examine the environmental toll of each in as much detail as we can and then build our choices back up again in the least impactful way we can find. Nothing that comes through our door is exempt.

We spent the first few years getting to grips with physical items before we gained the confidence to change the services we used or supported outside our home. We're still unravelling. We're pretty sure it will take us the rest of our lives.

When it all gets too complex, too controversial, when we seem to stumble in circles around conflicting information about just how damaging each approach is, we retreat to a simple three-pronged guide:

- Are we comfortable about how this item or service has reached us?
- Are we comfortable with its environmental impact while we use it?
- Are we comfortable about what happens to it afterwards?

We quickly realised that if we were happy with the answer to those three questions we wouldn't go far wrong. We really could significantly reduce the environmental impact of our everyday lives. We could take on the gnawing sense of impotence that seeps through every conversation, documentary and children's march. We could have an impact.

It takes time, commitment, and often a thick skin to ward off cynics who feel our approach is a judgement on their lives. It isn't. We know we don't have all the answers. We never will. We only know that we need to try to find them.

This book is not designed to berate us all for our environmental failings. In fact, the opposite is true. The overriding emotion on this huge, ongoing journey is one of empowerment – of snatching back an awareness, control and responsibility from an amoral global supply chain. This empowerment is heady and intoxicating.

We get a boost every time we step back from a subconscious decision or assumed behaviour in favour of a more sustainable solution. Whether that's looking past the pricey chlorine-washed lettuce in a plastic bag and picking up a cheaper whole one, or questioning the unchallenged authority of a global brand whose actions destroy primary rainforest.

We want to remove our financial backing, however modest, from those who destroy our planet, our health and our wallets. The truth is that those businesses aren't bent on global violation. It would be a whole lot easier if they were run by comic book villains stroking white cats, but environmental destruction is usually just collateral damage from the easiest, fastest, most profitable decisions. Companies can always lean on the convenient prop of 'consumer demand.'

Sure, we're told our actions will make no difference on a daily basis. But what's that overused but deliciously succinct phrase? '"It's only one plastic bag…," said seven billion people.'

❆ ❆ ❆

We're still learning, mostly because our day jobs aren't in environmental research. We're not hippies – incense makes me gag. And we're not hipsters either for that matter... although, full disclosure, my husband does have a beard. David is an engineer; I am a financial journalist. We earn almost exactly the national average for jobs that don't leave endless leisure time. We live in a semi. We didn't start all this from some privileged position where life mostly involved rearranging stonewashed linen for the perfect Instagram post or sauntering through a sun-drenched kitchen garden on a Tuesday afternoon while everyone else is at work.

We have the same pressures, the same concerns, the same levels of exhaustion on a Friday night and borderline dread on a Monday morning as everybody else. If we can do this, anyone can.

And more people than you might imagine are trying.

There are signs of an astonishing shift in attitude at the highest levels of economic power. All of a sudden, with investor sentiment experiencing a sea change and supply chains being threatened by climate change now (rather than some indistinct point in the future), we've woken up to the idea that a more sustainable approach is the only way to deliver long-term profitability.

In 2020 for example, as Australian forest fires burned and critically endangered species on sale as bushmeat in forgotten wet markets were believed to be the source of Covid-19, the geopolitical and economic meeting of the most powerful minds in the world at the World Economic Forum summit in Davos became a climate conference in all but name. The headline speaker wasn't a US president or Warren Buffet, it was Greta Thunberg.

In other words, sustainability isn't being discussed in a side room any longer. It is front and centre. I now can't have a conversation with anyone in the financial world without climate change coming up within the first few minutes. Greenwashing is becoming harder. This is all positive, powerful stuff that might just change an otherwise fatal future.

Back down here in the real world, we know our family is made up of just four microscopic lives. But we also know, now more than at any time since Beanbag Day, that we're part of a massive, surging, rising sea of millions of ordinary people demanding and achieving fundamental global change at an unprecedented speed.

We have been told for years now that we all have to make significant changes to our lives to prevent or at least slow climate change and our apocalyptic effects on the world. The problem is that we have been taking it all on board in fits and starts, with snippets of information passed on randomly, bordered by silence about everything else.

Nobody has actually sat us down and told us what the complete sustainability blueprint looks like as a whole, what our priorities need to be and what we tackle in what order to 'save the world.' How are we supposed to hang it all together in real life without having to decamp to an off-grid yurt? Is it even possible to enjoy the full richness of modern society, to raise our children within the wider communities that we love, on your average street, in your average town, without doing massive damage?

With no universal manual forthcoming, David and I and the kids went on a journey to find out. We needed to find out just how important all this really was to us. We needed to find out how far we could go.

2. Unravelling a Lifetime's Training

We went 'zero waste' overnight. We stopped using throwaway, single-use items and started using reusables for everything we brought into our home. In hindsight, it was a slightly stupid, instant, all-or-nothing decision.

Buying food that isn't wrapped in plastic was one of the hardest changes to make and it's fair to say we were spectacularly underprepared for the implications.

We were total wannabe foodies who enjoyed cooking but had fallen into the classic pasta sauce rut. We could make square meals from scratch but it was easier on a wet, dark Wednesday evening, when the kids were already climbing the walls, to grab something conveniently packaged that might pass for a healthy meal if we squinted.

Some kids somewhere must still grow up in lives where food shopping means visits to a series of quaint stores piled high with dry goods in hessian sacks or enormous cheeses personally sliced by an artisanal producer. Wax paper and loose veg must populate their memories of the typical food shop. It didn't in ours. Sure, we wandered curious round a farmer's market like the best of them, buying a few treats to savour. But that wasn't our real food shopping. That was aspirational sampling.

In the real world, we fed ourselves and our children from supermarkets. Taste, texture and nutrition were considerations that were outweighed by convenience, familiarity, perceptions of value and plastic-wrapped cleanliness.

Once a fortnight, we raced round a standard chain store, buying the same things we did the previous time thanks to well-honed brand recognition and aisle knowledge. We could have done the grocery shop in our sleep. In fact, I think we probably did, given the shocking sleeping habits of our children for several relentless years.

We would fill the boot of our diesel car with plastic bags full of plastic packs of food and drive home. There we would empty the last lot of identical, perfectly edible but 'passed its best' food into the compost and the plastic into the bin. Over and over again.

Over the next few days the metallic sound of the bin lid opening and closing would be an increasingly jarring part of the household noise. The tall metal cylinder perched at the edge of an already limited galley kitchen was used so frequently it felt like the focal point of our home.

The fridge, freezer and cupboards were rammed with branded convenience foods jam-packed with sugar, salt, preservatives and the rest. We wouldn't have ever said we were ready-meal reliant, we had even been known to make our own bread, but we were certainly that average UK family that throws away a third of the food it buys.

Sure, the aim was to eat everything we'd bought before going round in another circle, but we never reached that prize. I also thought the food I occasionally put into the bin would simply break down into benign organic matter in landfill. I was wrong. Rotting food in landfill produces one of the most potent greenhouse gases, methane. (Park the plastic for a second, if you want to make one easy change always compost your food waste. Every scrap.)

Then we decided to hurl a grenade into our slightly-fraught-but-generally-winging-it lives by cutting out every item that came wrapped in any plastic. It took three months from Bean-bag-Day to retrain our brains from all those autopilot purchases and associated behaviours and there were moments during the adjustment phase when I wondered if we were ever going to eat again.

Shopping now is very different – both in experience and cost. The first thing to disappear – by default – was the big supermarket shop. Try walking through one and finding a single display that doesn't have any plastic in it. It won't happen. Even, tragically, the fruit and veg with their own natural packaging and portioning, are remarkably difficult to find not encased in the stuff.

The problem with plastic

If you've picked up this book in the first place you're more than aware that our use of plastic is a problem. Quite how big of a problem though, is a difficult one for us mere mortals to appreciate. It's also being revised all the time, and not in a positive direction.

You only need to glimpse a few seconds of heartbreaking footage of huge decomposing whales whose stomach contents are almost entirely plastic or tiny sea bird chicks dying in agony from the bottle tops and nurdles their parents have mistaken for food to know that nature is having a nightmare.

So massive is the plastic pollution in our oceans that shocked sailors talk about travelling for days through the Great Pacific Garbage Patch – a monstrous collection of marine debris brought together by ocean currents in the

---

North Pacific. It's twice the size of France.

We often focus on the marine debris we can see — the majority of which is pollution originating on land, with fishing nets, dumped or lost shipping cargo and rubbish from oil rigs making up most of the rest.

Were you to swim underneath that patch — which wouldn't be a great idea — the water would be cloudy with microplastics. Microplastics are tiny fragments often just 5mm or smaller that are produced as larger pieces of plastic break down.

Pieces that small are also manufactured for microbeads in toothpaste and beauty products. Now banned in a handful of countries including the UK, millions of people either swallow or wash them straight down the drain on a daily basis. Too small to be picked up by filters or in treatment plants, they're pumped into our oceans in terrifying quantities.

As I write, new research has revealed there is twice as much microplastic in the world's oceans as scientists had previously thought.[27] Microplastics now outnumber zooplankton, the foundation for the marine food chain and a key player in climate regulation.

Ingested by organisms like shellfish, plankton and fish, microplastics can reduce feeding, fertility, growth and survival and can even change the behaviours of the marine life that gobbles it up.

That's before it makes its way up the food chain as smaller marine animals are eaten by larger predators, including humans. In other words, if you enjoy a shellfish supper or fish and chips on the way home from work, put tuna in the kids' sandwiches or simply use sea salt in your cooking, you're ingesting microplastics. To be honest, if you eat fish, cutting out the plastic seems like self preservation to me.

Plastic waste is worse on land than in oceans *Magda Ehlers, Pexels*

But that doesn't mean the rest of us are safe. In fact, the opposite is true. While the world is rapidly tuning into the horrific effect our plastic use and misuse is having on water, plastic in all its forms – like those polystyrene balls in our garden – causes plenty of problems on land.

In fact, scientists in Germany[28] have found that microplastic pollution is between four and 23 times higher on land than it is in the oceans, depending on the environment. And, just like in water, microplastics on land are putting the ecosystems they pollute and the life those environments support – including humans – in 'serious jeopardy,' the study warned. Remember about Bisphenol A leaching toxins? Think of that on a massive scale.

Alongside evidence of microplastics in the blood of sea turtles, the latest study to rock our view of plastic pollution has found microplastics in the blood of farm animals including cows and pigs, leading to fears over how they move through the food chain, including building up deposits in human organs and breastmilk. Meanwhile, studies into microplastics in drinking water are ongoing.

Looking down a suburban street on recycling day, you'd be forgiven for thinking we're on top of the plastic recycling game. We're not. Barely 9% of the plastic we have produced so far is recycled or even incinerated. The rest, if it isn't shoved into the ocean, is dumped into landfill where it can leach into the soil and water – impacting everything that drinks the water or feeds from the land.

There are other threats from this man-made pollution, too. They range from the risk of microplastic surfaces carrying diseases into our soil to breaking down even further to become such small nanoplastics that they can cross cell walls and other membranes in living organisms such as the placenta or the blood brain barrier. Studies on fish suggest the effect can be so extreme that it can cause brain damage and change behaviour.[29]

The unnerving truth, though, is that there's a massive knowledge gap about just how microplastics affect the human body and impact human health.

Do I literally have plastic on the brain? Do my children? Do yours? The sickening truth is probably. When this all dawned on me, half an hour before tea time, I went into our kitchen horrified that everything I was about to put in front of them, even the air they were breathing at that very moment and in every moment to come, could be tainted. I wanted to snatch up the kids and run away to somewhere safe and unpolluted, but there's nowhere to go. Nowhere to get away from it.

You can't even escape to some pristine mountaintop. According to one study, the French Pyrenees are littered with microplastics and 365 new pieces rain down on every square metre, every day.

So what are we doing about plastic pollution? Actually, very little. Ignore the eco marketing spin, because despite the growing anti-plastic sentiment, seven of the ten big UK supermarkets are increasing single-use plastic packaging.

Collectively, we're now using around 900,000 tonnes of plastic that does a single job for a few days before being thrown away every year.[6]

The UK Government is 'working towards' a series of 'ambitions' and 'targets' of eliminating avoidable plastic waste by the end of 2042. 2042? Another two decades of continuing as we are?

Stop the plastic ride, we were getting off. We wanted no part in this hidden nightmare. Who cares how socially uncomfortable that makes our food shopping. Which it can be. I'm pretty sure handing a metal container over to a grumpy middle-aged bloke at a deli counter is one of the most intimidating activities known to man.

And sometimes it doesn't work anyway. We have a standard spiel designed to explain that we don't buy things in plastic, so could you just put the food straight into the box please. The person will listen politely, sometimes nod, sometimes mutter, and then reach for several plastic sheets or cling film to wrap the item in before depositing it in our box. We'll stop them, explain again, they'll nod again and put the plastic in their hand straight into the bin. We'd have caused more unnecessary plastic waste, not less.

Ignore the corporate chat about encouraging customers to bring our own containers to reduce plastic use, most of the time these are transactions that leave us apologising in the most British of ways for being a customer. To be honest, I quite often avoid these purchases altogether because six times out of ten it's a disheartening and depressing experience. Luckily others aren't.

These days, our standard food shop means taking a bunch of empty glass jars and battered old cotton bags to a couple of small independent shops within walking distances of our high street. We clink our way in, weigh out the goods we need straight into our own containers – from spaghetti and oil to cereal and sweets – and head home again.

When we first made the switch, the weighing and measuring seemed to take forever compared with the striplight efficiency of the check-out. But there's also a chat and a sense of community there too.

We know people's names. They know ours. Our children are slipped little handfuls of sweets while we're busy purchasing sensible things.

We started buying fruit and veg loose from an actual greengrocer and milk in glass bottles that were left on our doorstep to be collected and refilled by a milkman. I hadn't realised they all still existed until we went looking for them. It all feels a bit old school, but it's the way we all shopped until relatively recently. Single-use plastic only really went mainstream in the 1950s and 1960s – within living memory. I certainly remember the rattling of the pre-dawn milk rounds from early childhood, the invention of plastic encased microwave-able ready meals in the 1980s, and the arrival of salad in a bag in the mid-1990s. I was pretty sure paying more for someone to chop up your lettuce would never catch on.

My mum and dad can easily recall the days of string bags, paper cones and being handed ice-cold chocolate straight from the freezing meat locker as a reward for being patient in the butcher's. In fact, my dad still can't countenance sweet treats at room temperature. And if you'd have told my granny that I was writing a book about how we live without plastic, she'd have been astonished. For more than half of her life that was the norm.

When we explain we don't have a bin because we don't create any waste, most people look at us with bemusement before asking how that's even possible. I do sometimes suspect they think we're just massive hoarders with a gigantic pile of concealed rubbish. We're not, but nor have we invented some miraculous new way of life. We've just reverted back.

I was once told we were 'regressing just to prove a point.' It was early days, at a point when the efforts we were making felt ridiculous, futile and that all they did was to create distance between us and our friends. I was hurt by that statement at the time – made by a woman who has since made concerted efforts to cut out plastic herself – but I guess it's now a badge of honour.

Those first months of zero waste were a bit chaotic and emotional, though. And of course it wasn't just about breaking the 'big shop' habits either. There were definitely a few times when we'd grab a packet of Quavers at lunchtime or a snack to placate the kids on a long journey and not realise what we'd done for hours afterwards. When it finally dawned on us, those feelings of impotence and ridiculousness flooded back.

It didn't help that there was still a kind of legacy plastic in our home. That's what those Insta lifestyle gurus don't tell you, what to do with all the plastic that has already seeped in – the Tupperware and takeaway boxes kept for the batch cooking plans that somehow never quite happen, or the handful of disposable forks you snatched at the till on the lunchtime sandwich run just in case.

When they realised we were serious about all this, some friends and family started playing a game of find-the-plastic whenever they came round to ours, rifling through cupboards and randomly opening drawers.

They'll still find some, too. Throwing reusable plastic like Tupperware out once it's there is pointless anyway. You can't ever get rid of plastic – that's the whole problem – so once it has been manufactured and paid for, however long ago, the best, most sustainable thing to do is to use it as much as possible before recycling it only when it's no longer fit for purpose.[7]

That was the idea behind the now spurned plastic bag in the first place. It was designed to be used over and over again – a more environmentally friendly option to the paper wrapping we'd been using in the UK since 1310, according to some records. So many centuries' worth of paper is a lot of trees, water and energy, and it was a problem Sten Gustaf Thulin was trying to solve when he came up with the plastic bag in 1959.

He meant it to be reused many times, not thrown away after carrying a single item a tiny distance just once. No wonder British shoppers used more than two billion plastic bags in 2020. In fact the slender resources involved in production of plastic bags, compared with paper and cotton mean you'd have to use a paper bag at least three times, and a cotton tote around 131 times, to offset the land, water, energy and paper demands of their production.

As novice 'zero wasters' we had also dipped our toe into the world of biodegradable materials as a plastic alternative which, it turned out, wasn't a problem-free solution either.

Preparing for our first post-plastic party, and still believing everything that labelled itself eco-friendly actually was, I'd gone searching for alternatives to plastic cups to supplement our glasses and found biodegradable ones. These, I happily read, would naturally break down, unlike plastic. They had the same look, the same feel, they performed the same booze-containing task. The job, as they say, was a good 'un.

The party went well, we drank too many sticky apricot-coloured cocktails and subjected at least one guest to our terrible homemade cider while avoiding it ourselves. No, the problems began with the clear-up.

I had understood that the biodegradable label meant the item quickly collapsed into natural components when composted. In fact, biodegradable bags can still carry a full load after having been buried in soil for three years.[8]

If something is biodegradable, its component molecules break down naturally into water, naturally occurring gases and biomass, but there are no hard and fast timescales involved. It can hang around for years.

There are stricter rules on packaging sold as compostable. It has to break down into organic matter within 12 weeks, but only under industrial conditions, which you don't often find in your garden compost heap. But at least these will all eventually become natural matter.

Compostable bags that will indeed break down in your own worm-filled pile at home are thankfully labelled as such.

Then there are the slippery oxo-biodegradable materials some-times even referred to as bioplastics. These are made in the same way that normal, fossil-based, petrochemical plastic is, just with some additives added that make it react with oxygen and eventually break down – into tiny pieces of plastic.[9]

There are now all sorts of efforts underway to try to clarify and help consumers understand the differences, including an EU ban on oxo-biodegradable materials from 2021, though the UK, de-spite voting for the EU ban, has yet to confirm similar legislation post-Brexit.[10]

But back then, we didn't happen to have a relevant PhD to help us unravel all this and were using 'biodegradable,' 'compostable' and 'bioplastic' interchangeably with no clear idea of the difference.

It was becoming increasingly, alarmingly, clear that if we want-ed to do more good than harm, we couldn't rely on information we were being fed. The changes we made and actions we took needed to be backed up by some hardcore research of our own. Meanwhile, I had smugly chucked all that 'biodegradable' party paraphernalia on our compost heap only to have to recover it later. I vowed from that moment to understand what we were buying.

3. Assume Nothing

At first, we just tried to replicate our old eating habits. But our zero waste approach meant that pizzas, crisps, chocolate bars, yoghurt, ice cream, butter, pre-portioned fish, meat and cheese, factory-made quiches, cakes, pastries, cereal and bread were off the family menu along with another hundred things that didn't even register as plastic wrapped until we went to pick them up. Takeaways, too, became all but impossible.

'How are we going to find [fill in the blank] not wrapped in plastic?' was a question that came up endlessly. So we had a go at churning our own butter. We had found a local dairy and got them to fill up one of our containers with cream. I appreciate that sounds like something straight out of *Larkrise to Candleford* but there happens to be a commercial dairy on the outskirts of our town.

Butter is ridiculously easy to make and I'll hold my hands up to admit I did spend a day smugly lost in the domesticity of it all. Snipping rosemary from the harangued-looking pot on the windowsill to go in your own home-churned butter must be a massive adulting tick. But once we'd 'processed' (for which read 'whacked the mixer on') 30 litres of cream, filled the freezer and typed 'butter paddles' into a well-known search engine in a fit of romantic idiocy, the exercise has never been repeated – not least because being-elbow deep in that amount of fat put me right off dairy for weeks.

Luckily there are plenty of very easy makes that are far easier and tastier. Making yoghurt in a slow cooker, for example, was a bit of a revelation that secured my husband David regular bragging points. A slow cooker is an all-enclosed pan that gently cooks food for hours.

❋ ❋ ❋

Then there's peanut butter, which requires little more alchemy than mushing said nut in a food processor for 30 seconds. The taste is infinitely better, especially if you can be bothered to roast them first and toss a bit of salt into the mix.

When it dawned on us, painfully slowly, that we could do this with any nut we could possibly conceive of the gloves were off. Hazelnut spread – that's all I'm saying. We're never paying through the nose for the inferior, shop-bought variety again on taste alone.

And during lockdown, when pasta was so hard to get hold of supermarket employees were bribed to reveal delivery times, being able to make spaghetti by getting the kids to swish an egg in a bit of flour for a fraction of the price stopped us losing the will to live at least once. Even if it then took three days to get uncooked dough off the kitchen floor. (It's right up there with dried-on Weetabix, which must surely be the hardest substance on earth.)

Buoyed by some simple homemade wins we started venturing further into the world of culinary switches. On the whole it was fun, interesting and informative – even when things got a bit out of hand.

When our daughter's 5th birthday came around, she chose to take 20 of her friends and family to a nearby woodland thankfully set up for such things, with rope swings, obstacle courses, hideouts and the concluding campfire, which naturally required marshmallows. So along with the cake and its decorations, the rolls and what seemed to be a hundred other things, including the ketchup, we set about making them from scratch – inevitably at 2am the night before the party.

By 2.02am we'd realised that following a single recipe for marshmallows was the easy bit because the ingredients themselves only came in plastic. So we had to make those first. This wasn't cooking from scratch, it was cooking from minus scratch.

Slow cooker yoghurt

Making yoghurt in a slow cooker is time consuming but easy. You'll need 50ml of plain yoghurt (bought or kept from an earlier batch) for every litre of milk used. Plant-based yoghurt can be made using a similar process, with a thickener like tapioca or agar, and a probiotic or non-dairy 'starter' yoghurt.

Vlad Chețan, Pexels

First, the milk goes into a slow cooker on 'high' or 'max' temperature. When it hits 82°C after 2-3 hours, turn off the cooker and cool to 40°C. Thin the yoghurt with a little of the warm milk before stirring it thoroughly into the slow cooker.

Next, though it seems like a weird thing to do, wrap the cooker in a thick towel or, at a push, lots of tea towels to provide consistent insulation. You want to bring the temperature down very slowly so the mixture sets. A thinner set for plain yoghurt will take 9-10 hours, but a greek-style effort is probably closer to 12-13. You could even strain the mix in a cheese cloth. Play with the timings a little to get the ideal set. The end result will keep in the fridge for a couple of weeks. Bon appétit

---

The result was frankly useless if you expected to impale it on a stick and wave it at a heat source. But at least one child said our homemade marshmallows were the best they'd tasted. We were too exhausted to care. But receiving praise from a four-year-old about sugar disguised as a cloud wasn't the only benefit we started to enjoy by cooking everything freshly.

The obvious bonus is that we know exactly what is in it all. There's no hidden sugar, salt or fat. It's also amazing how little bread or cake or cheese or yoghurt you eat when you have to work up the energy to make it first. We tended to only eat a dollop of ice cream because we couldn't plead ignorance over the sheer quantity of sugar and fat that went into it. Coupled with a lack of shop-bought snacks and chocolate, David and I lost several pounds in the first year.

❋ ❋ ❋

Wrestling out of the firm grip of the supermarkets has had other, unexpected benefits, too.

It's undoubtedly cheaper to cook from scratch, especially if you can batch cook and fill every available space in your oven to reduce energy costs. The need to become the more organised, list-writing type of shoppers has also helped dramatically cut our food waste. We're lucky that we can and do buy our raw ingredients from small, independent retailers that source from nearby suppliers and growers and pass on our questions about sustainability, sometimes even with enthusiasm.

But what we hadn't anticipated were the indirect effects of a brand vacuum. If you ever pop round to ours and start randomly opening our kitchen cupboards, fridge or freezer they would probably remind you of a blind taste test or an episode of the BBC's *Eat Well for Less*. There's definitely food in there, but it's all in label-less jars, paper bags or sometimes even sacks for bulk items like bread flour and oats. At first, visitors find the lack of familiar packaging quite unsettling. We get a lot of questions that start: 'Is this proper/ real/like…?' as guests hold jars up to the light with badly disguised scepticism.

On the plus side, our children now have zero pester power. We don't need to navigate the snack shuffle at the supermarket check-out because they have no hope of deploying the 'It's not the one I like' argument at mealtimes. Nor, for that matter, have the adults.

Not everything has switched quite so well to either a homemade or non-plastic alternative though, and four years in, tea remains a surprisingly tense subject in our house. Few people realise that the packaging isn't the only plastic problem. The average home-brewed tea bag is up to 30% plastic thanks to the polypropylene used to hold it together.

We submerge these things in boiling water before robustly straining them and drinking the whole thing down. Depending on the type of bag involved, we're ingesting an incredible 11.6 billion microplastic and 3.1 billion nanoplastic particles[11] per bag. And the British drink more than 60 billion cups of tea a year.

Thankfully, like so many other products and services, the grow-ing discontent over the use of plastic has forced the hand of those who produce our favourite brews. A couple of brands supplying the UK market are now rolling out plastic-free tea bags, but it's re-markably difficult to work out if they are in your favourite brand. And if all you can think about when you stare into your cup is how many microplastics you're about to sip down, I'd imagine you'd want to know.

Needless to say we lost the taste for teabags pretty quickly and switched to loose leaf – with unconvincing results. It turns out those blends we're all brought up on are remarkably difficult to replicate. While I'm more of a coffee drinker, David started blowing out his

Palm oil: a wildlife serial killer

We also know our food doesn't contain preservatives, additives or, thankfully, any trace of the palm oil found in around half of all supermarket products. Palm oil comes from the fruit of the African palm oil tree, which is now grown all over the world.

It is the cheap, useful ingredient that helps keep your spread spreadable, your lipstick applicable, your doughnuts springy and your shampoo gloopy. You find it in ice cream, crackers, bread, chocolate, detergent, soap, the list goes on.

Palm oil is in half of all supermarket products. And it's directly responsible for the massive, relentless destruction of some of the world's most diverse habitats: tropical rainforests. Huge areas of these complex, carbon-sinking ecosystems are cleared, often illegally, to make way for palm tree plantations.

The existing trees, particularly in countries like Malaysia and Indonesia, are cut down and vegetation burned, simultaneously adding greenhouse gases into the atmosphere while removing the trees that reduce them.

Once the tree grows too high for the fruit to be easily picked the palm itself is also chopped down and new ones grown. The effect on already endangered wildlife is apocalyptic. Tigers, rhinos, elephants, and tens of thousands of orangutans have been killed or have died as a direct result of the quest for palm oil.[30] Seeing footage of one orangutan hitting a bulldozer engine in a desperate attempt to stop it ripping apart the last corner of forest on a recent BBC documentary made me feel physically sick. And so it should.

By 2016 around 75% of the total palm oil imports to the UK were considered sustainable, but it seems that is far from the panacea manufacturers and retailers would have us believe.

Palm oil production has decimated orangutans   Pixabay, Pexels

In fact, it could be making it worse.

One 15-year-long study of more than 2,200 licensed palm growing areas using everything from satellite imagery and government reports to palm oil companies' own data, found that plantations with sustainable certification have lost 38% of their forest cover since 2007 compared with 34% of non-certified land.[31] In other words, the use of sustainable labels has facilitated the expansion of plantations, destroying even more carbon-absorbing forests in southeast Asia.

The palm oil industry points to other research that suggest slightly lower rates among certified plantations, but all show deforestation. 'If you need to produce palm oil, you need to remove forest. That's what we're seeing,' said Professor Roberto Gatti, a research associate at the University of Purdue's Department of Forestry and Natural Resources, and the study's lead author, when the report was released in 2018.

'Our research shows quite unequivocally that, unfortunately, there is no way to produce sustainable palm oil that did not come from deforestation, and that the claims by corporations, certification schemes and non government organisations are simply 'greenwashing,' useful to continue business as usual,' he told the *Independent* at the time. 'No shortcuts: if you use palm oil, certified or not, you are definitely destroying tropical forests.'

'We should be conscious of our use of products with palm oil and consider alternatives such as rapeseed, canola, flaxseed and sunflower. We lived for many centuries without palm oil. We can certainly do it again,' he urged.

Others have a different approach though, particularly when it comes to supporting small scale farmers trying to make a difference on the ground. These days, a 'deforestation free' label has emerged to support them and the environment. But deforestation-free is really hard to guarantee, not least because the supply chain is complex and difficult to trace.

I'm just relieved that we don't have to try to navigate all this because we don't need palm oil anyway.

Palm oil by another name...		
	Vegetable Oil	Palm Stearine
	Vegetable Fat	Palmitoyl Oxostearamide
	Palm Kernel	Palmitoyl Tetrapeptide-3
	Palm Kernel Oil	Sodium Laureth Sulfate
	Palm Fruit Oil	Sodium Lauryl Sulfate
	Palmate	Sodium Kernelate
	Palmitate	Sodium Palm Kernelate
	Palmolein	Sodium Lauryl
	Glyceryl	Lactylate/Sulphate
	Stearate	Hydrated Palm Glycerides
	Stearic Acid	Ethyl Palmitate
	Elaeis Guineensis	Octyl Palmitate
	Palmitic Acid	Palmityl Alcohol.[32]

cheeks when I offered to put the kettle on, muttering tragically: 'I don't really want that tea, thanks.'

I knew what he meant and it wasn't just a complaint about tea. We'd already changed so much about how we consumed, made life that bit more complicated and stressful with every snack or meal-time in pursuit of zero waste. What he was actually saying was: 'Are we really becoming so extreme about all this that we're depriving ourselves of an enjoyable cuppa too?'

We seemed to be setting ourselves up as 'other' – excluding ourselves from basic activities like making a cup of tea, or ordering a takeaway, or picking up a snack from the corner shop – tiny life-smoothing luxuries enjoyed by everyone else we knew.

We choose not to do those things. And for what exactly? If you stop smoking or cut back on the cake, or cycle to work rather than get the bus you get immediate personal benefits. The change in behaviour, especially if it involves sustained effort, gives you something back. It's often quantifiable too – you can see the numbers on the scales or your personal best on a run change.

But our lifestyle changes weren't ever going to do that. We hadn't even managed to eliminate microplastics from the little patch of earth we had full management over, let alone personally protect the last remaining rainforests of Africa, or South East Asia or South America.

We had to get our heads around the fact that, aside from the knowledge that we didn't need to do the bin dash to the kerb moments before the truck arrived, there would never be a way to quantify our overall progress. At no point would we be able to turn to the people who told us we were too insignificant to make a difference and say 'Look at this, though – we have made this difference.'

All we could do, like the smoker or dieter or fitness convert, was to wait for the ridiculously first world sense of deprivation to transition to normal and then to the daily buzz of empowerment.

Very quickly it became clear that if these changes were to last they had to be emotionally positive. We embraced the fact that every purchasing decision we made about anything – particularly when the decision was not to purchase at all – was a step towards or away from the kind of world we want to live in.

When the messages we are bombarded with are either that we should carry on as before and that someone else will surely sort all this out, that we as consumers must be guilted into saving the planet, or that the situation is hopeless, those decisions have to remain positive and proactive. Every time. And for us they usually are.

We're still working on a brew solution though and frankly we've got to the point where we hope guests will just go straight for the wine to save us the embarrassment. But pretty soon the niggle about tea was washed away by some far bigger challenges.

We had thought cutting out the plastic might be quite straightforward, a black and white decision to make and a well-defined change to adopt before striding off into the new eco-friendly dawn. It hadn't been. And now it was becoming unnervingly clear as we settled into a new normal that we'd only really got on top of the easy bit.

So far we had taken a simple, visually clear criterion and applied it universally. We bought food that wasn't sold in plastic and didn't buy food that was. Tick.

But what about the food itself? What had happened before it got to us, and how did we feel about the impact of that journey?

We were starting to realise that making the journey was leading to more questions than answers, more grey areas, misinformation and conflicts of interest than we ever imagined – and that was just about food. We hadn't even got started on anything else that came into our home yet.

Take a single, uncontroversial ingredient, let's say peppers. Should we buy them grown in a UK hothouse or ones trucked in from Spain? What if the Spanish ones are organic? Or the only UK option is wrapped in plastic? Which is better for the environment? Or at least less harmful? If we ever want to eat peppers again without negatively impacting the planet in some way are we going to have to grow our own? Because self-sufficiency wasn't really part of the plan....

All we could do was dive in and hope we didn't drown in the detail as we swam around looking for food that worked for us and the planet. We started with the problem of transport because food mileage was a well established measure that meant we could actually make some decisions based on numbers for once. Or, at least, we thought we could.

Three quarters of all the fruit and veg now eaten in the UK is imported. Almost all the fruit we eat has been grown overseas, and soft fruit in particular is flown in. It turns out that the UK only produces half of all the food that is consumed on these shores – which is somewhat patriotically disconcerting as well as practically unsustainable.

Global sourcing is not a new approach to feeding a nation. One of our family stories is the recollection of the first banana my great uncle ever tasted after the Second World War, shipped from the other side of the world and unloaded onto the Liverpool docks. We were very aware that bananas came from overseas.

But the fact that such a vast proportion of the apples eaten in Britain are imported from South Africa, or at best France, when the fruit grows very well in the miles of orchards you can see from the motorway near our house seemed to be absurd.

The obvious solution appeared to be only to buy food produced not just in the UK but as close to our immediate vicinity as possible.

That immediately threw up two questions.

The first we were becoming increasingly familiar with. Were we really prepared to give up things we took great pleasure in for the sake of an unquantifiable, but undoubtedly minuscule effect? Or even just to settle for not adding to the runaway levels of damage that our disconnected food shop was causing each and every day?

We are children of the 90s. We grew up safe in the knowledge that the world's produce was at our fingertips at any time of the year. When we were kids, cuisine was regularly valued on the exoticism of its ingredients. Even if your palate was resolutely British, a Sunday roast at an ageing auntie's always included the smug mention that the family was consuming lamb imported from the other side of the world.

Even in our twenties, the craze for exotic bottled water shipped, plastic encased, in vast quantities from tropical islands thousands of miles away, packed a serious economic punch. And then there's the avocado – a native of Mexico and now all but a dictionary definition of the British Millennial. We had come of age and then brought our children into the world on the assumption that it was normal to buy exotic food cheaply all year round. Things were clearly going to have to change, starting with my obsession with avocado on toast.

But the second question was whether a straightforward food mile approach was even a worthwhile aim. When I put the question of food miles to Riverford Organic Farmers, the sustainably produced veg box people, they told me that for most of the year our carbon impact would be smaller if we bought organic tomatoes trucked in from Spain than those heated thanks to fossil fuels in a UK hothouse.

That means the answer has to be to eat food grown in the UK at the time of year it is traditionally produced. We finally arrived at a robust solution – seasonal, native eating.

But by now the scene in the movie *Notting Hill* where the fruitarian is quizzed mercilessly on her insanely restrictive diet by a bunch of disbelieving yuppies was playing on a loop in my head. Forget our own cooking for a second, at this rate we'd never be invited out for so much as a light snack ever again. More importantly, how would we ever separate the kids from bananas without them leaving home forever?

As the easy eco-wins began to run out, we started realising we'd have to layer up the environmental criteria if we wanted to avoid greenwashing our own lives. And there was still so much more to get our teeth into.

Within twelve months of Beanbag Day our aim was to buy food that wasn't wrapped in plastic, that had the lowest possible food miles we could find, that was seasonal and, if in any way possible without breaking the bank, organic in a bid to reduce the impact of pesticides, herbicides and weed killers on both the environment and our own bodies.

This couldn't be a one-off experiment. We have to keep working to make it happen every week, in every month, of every year.

Today, if we can't source the ingredients we need from the UK we'll go as far as Western Europe if necessary. But I'll hold my hands up to the exceptions. Those are tea, coffee, some spices, 'small amounts' of chocolate and an occasional, and much reduced, bunch of those tasty bananas.

I later found out that because they're light on packaging, grown in natural conditions without hothousing and transported those long distances by boat, not to mention the fact that they pack a decent nutritional punch, they're far from the biggest villain of the global food supply world – coming in at around 110g C02e each [see the next box for an explanation of C02e].[12]

Which is a relief, sort of. But if I want avocado on toast at this rate I'll still have to grow it first. Unfortunately that hopeful-looking sprouting seed on the windowsill won't be supplying breakfast for another decade.

But none of this had even acknowledged the true elephant (or should that be cow?) in the room, our relationship with animal products. I'd always been vegetarian, but David comes from traditional farming stock where historically, no meal is without meat, let alone dairy products.

And yet these days our entire household has fallen into a committed flexitarian [see box], if not quite full time vegan diet.

Changing your diet can have a big impact   Vie Studio, Pexels

Going flexi: the climate case

We think of climate change as happening somewhere else, some dense rainforest containing animals and cultures so different from our own that we can put them in a box marked, at best, 'unfamiliar' and walk away. We can comfortably blame the people of India for using too many wood-fuelled stoves, or Indonesia for relying so heavily on plastic without recycling facilities. But carbon emissions per head of the population are far higher in western nations – usually because of overeating and overconsuming in general, particularly the intake of dairy and meat products.

Life on earth is based on carbon. But too much carbon floating about in the atmosphere, rather than captured in plants, animals, fungi and the like, traps heat, warming the planet.

Measuring our carbon emissions as individuals, or even discussing the greenhouse gases released as part of a specific process, doesn't ever seem to be done consistently – which is a total pain in the neck if you're trying to compare the figures.

Some calculations include indirect emissions in the total, coming from, for example, the fuel burned to ship a component to a factory to be made into a car or trousers. Others only start the clock from the point of completion, purchase or use. So the numbers vary wildly. I've tried to always take as full a picture of all this as possible, basing my approach on that of Mike Berners-Lee, the carbon counting king. So if you've seen estimates of the average Briton's annual footprint reported as both 13 tonnes of CO_2e and 6 tonnes of CO_2e, that's why.

The e bit, which stands for 'equivalent,' is important too. We describe our 'carbon' footprint and obsess over 'carbon' emissions, but we're actually talking about a wider mix of greenhouse gases in this shorthand – carbon dioxide, methane, nitrous oxide and refrigerant gases – including the CFCs and alike that *Blue Peter* warned us about in the 1980s.

In general, scientists and everyone else use the terms 'carbon emissions' and 'carbon footprint' as shorthand for

More nuts and grains and less meat   Frans van Heerden, Pexels

the full range of greenhouse gases including CO_2, methane (at least 28 times as more problematic as CO_2 over its lifetime and far worse in the first few years after release), nitrous oxide (hundreds of times more potent than CO_2) and refrigerant gases (many thousand times worse).

In terms of the cocktail we're producing, UK emissions impacting on climate comprise roughly 80% CO_2, 11% methane, 5% nitrous oxide and 3% everything else, including those refrigerant gases.[33]

It's obvious that land plays a crucial role in the climate change story. Half of all the habitable land in the world is now used for agriculture. That seems like an extraordinary amount, especially when it turns out that 77% of that agricultural land is used for livestock and animal feed production but provides just 18% of the global calorie supply.[34]

While agriculture, forestry and similar land use make up a quarter of human greenhouse gas emissions, land in a natural state absorbs carbon dioxide equivalent to a third of those emitted from fossil fuels and industrial activity.

And the system doesn't work anyway. Two billion people are overweight and food waste is gargantuan, and yet more than 820 million are malnourished.

The European Commission warns in no uncertain terms that: '[t]he average Western diet with high intakes of meat, fat and sugar is a risk for individual health, social systems and the environmental life support systems.'[35]

Even before the Intergenerational Panel on Climate Change at the United Nations came up with the advice that would later be coined a flexitarian diet, it was clear the way this needed to go in our house. Less meat, less dairy, smaller portions in general.

> Specifically, a sustainable diet that would use resources at rates that do not exceed the capacity of the Earth to replace them means one 'high in coarse grains, pulses, fruits and vegetables, and nuts and seeds; low in energy-intensive animal-sourced and discretionary foods (such as sugary beverages); and with a carbohydrate threshold.'

So sadly we couldn't just replace cheese or steak with our body weight in chips. Which was a blow.

For a long time, though, that's the way I thought about eco-eating. I made the classic dieter's mistake of thinking about all this in terms of what I was losing. But it turns out a decent flexitarian diet is one that adds foods. Things that we'd never thought of, that we'd skipped over, that we didn't have a clue what to do with.

But even if, as a consuming nation, we each substitute just one meat-based meal in an entire week's worth of food for a vegan option we could reduce our total greenhouse gas emissions by more than 8%. That's huge – the equivalent of taking 16 million cars off the road. And all achieved through a single meal swap that saves us cash at the same time.

Thousands of people are doing far better than that, though. Whether it was for their health, environmental concerns or a bit of both, half a million people signed up to Veganuary last year, twice the number that made the pledge the year before. And they're just the ones that made a formal pledge on a website. Everyone we know just went for it. As did we.

Meat and dairy products in our house are now the treat they should be, not least – I'll happily admit – because organic, high welfare meat and dairy is rightly expensive, yoghurt comes in plastic cartons or emissions-heavy glass and butter comes in non-compostable wrappers and we've already discussed churning your own.[13]

Coming from a farming background, David has always tried hard to avoid cheap meat. But including animal products in an average of just one meal a week means we can focus on spending that little bit more when and increasingly if we do invest in meat, fish, poultry or dairy in order to support organic, regenerative agricultural practices.

Meanwhile, we started exploring a rich new world of textures and tastes that we had always assumed was reserved for trendy people. But we hit a snag.

I hugely admire those people who have been able to look at their diet, especially if it had once been a traditional Western one, and turned it on its head to embrace plants to the absolute exclusion of all else for environmental, ethical and health reasons. All power to them. I'm trying to be one of them.

But so many of the meat and dairy-free alternatives to the classics you find on the market are encased in plastic or come in cartons with an internal plastic film.

Ticking the plant-based box doesn't exempt us from the same what and how of the ingredients themselves either. Those weirdly aggressive anti-vegans usually use the example of almond milk to illustrate why they think vegans are yet another bunch of greenwashers and therefore, they may hope, no threat to their meat-eating existence.

They have a point. Almond milk production may involve a fraction of the carbon produced by the equivalent quantity of semi-skimmed. But the water and chemical treatment it demands is colossal, it is grown thousands of miles away, usually in California, as a monoculture that does nothing for local biodiversity, and is even linked to the devastation of bee populations. That's before you start thinking about creating and shipping the plastic lined, difficult-to-recycle carton all the way from the West Coast of America.

After a bit of experimentation we found we could thankfully avoid most of those mind-bending rabbit holes because it's very easy to make your own non-dairy alternatives – within reason.

Vegan 'chease' can be whipped up from (less destructively produced) nuts including native walnuts, herbs and a bit of salt in a blender. Our homemade oat milk is one part oats to four parts water, blitzed for 30 seconds and passed through an old and – god willing – clean T-shirt. The UK is a serious oat producer so it's also native, cheap as chips and widely available as an organic ingredient. Plus oat production is really light on water use.

That's not the end of the controversy. Once we started digging into the realities of other large scale production processes alarms began to sound.

Many people are aware of the devastating impact of trawling for tiger or jumbo prawns before they are shipped across the world. But what about olive oil, which can be a particularly sinister customer?

Such is the demand for this elixir of life that many commercial olive harvests are nothing like the bucolic images of wily old Nonnas halfway up a ladder having a whale of a time while teasing off the odd fruit in a picturesque grove.

Each season around the Mediterranean trees are instead harvested at night by hoovering olives off trees, along with millions of legally protected songbirds. Hardest hit are some of the UK's best loved birds – robins, wagtails, greenfinches to name just a few.

And yet you'll see bog standard olive oil on the tables of otherwise environmentally aware households across the world. It once had such a place in our house that there's a permanent ring on the wooden worktop.

If you go looking, and I mean really hunting, there is a tiny handful of organic, hand-picked or mechanically harvested olive oil out there in glass bottles. But it is pricey. In the meantime though, getting to grips with the true nature of the typical olive harvest was yet another reminder of the strange, implied validation bestowed on ingredients that prominently line the shelves of our high street food shops and out of town supermarkets.

We switched to UK-grown rapeseed oil. Even the top end cold-pressed choices are far cheaper than comparable olive oils, though we're still looking for an organic version that doesn't come in plastic.

I wonder if that's why so many of us were so horrified by recent revelations about the number of British supermarket coconut products that were picked by monkeys in chains. Public outcry saw them rapidly snatched from the shelves along with fervent promises to do better.

But that's the problem. We had all assumed these and other household names were already doing better, that standard practice includes checking our food isn't dependent on exploitation of man, beast or ecosystem. It doesn't. So we have to keep doing it for ourselves until they get the message. Fine by me.

Changing our shopping habits, unearthing different recipes, finding viable alternatives to deeply harmful or plastic-wrapped products shipped in from the other side of the world leaving environmental chaos in their wake has been genuinely fun, fascinating and – that word again – empowering.

We've finally dug ourselves out of the kind of bread, pasta, cheese, fish finger, meat curry diet we had fallen into while we were concentrating on other things. Our food repertoire is wider, better for our health and our wallets.

Cue a bit more weight loss, cash recovery and – always a bonus – no incriminating wrappers. I used to eye people who snacked on 'rabbit food' with suspicion but so help me, it turns out sunflower seeds and walnuts are more than acceptable, though obviously they're better washed down with a decent glug of English wine.

Crucially, acknowledging the true cost of the 21st Century approach to food production has led us to reduce the sheer quantity of food in our home, on our plates and, above all, in our compost. With food production of all kinds responsible for a quarter of the globe's greenhouse gas emissions,[14] I suspect that it may be the most impactful decision we have made.

4. Down the Drain

We knew a few things would change when we went zero but we hadn't expected our sense of smell would be one of them.

We are all bombarded by strong smells everyday but they've become such an intrinsic part of our lives that for the most part, we either don't notice them or, oddly, actively pursue them.

Take that 'new car' smell for example, the one in itself reminiscent of the 'Saturday afternoon at a major electrical retailer' scent. It is so closely associated with big purchase satisfaction that it's practically Pavlovian. Breathe in deeply and you too will be transported to a zen-like state of personal fulfilment and success via a car showroom – a place where you are winning at life to such an extent that you can definitely afford the upgrade package. Now open your wallet.

But that smell is the result of offgassing, which sounds like a bodily function but is in fact the result of materials like the thermoplastics in car interiors curing and changing temperature during the manufacturing process. Solvents, paints, even leather all boost the toxic bouquet. Together, the mix of 'bromine, chlorine, lead, formaldehyde and other substances known to be carcinogens, allergens, and endocrine disruptors in seat cushions, arm rests, floor coverings, steering wheels, instrument panels, and other interior components'[15] first revealed in 2006, can cause shortness of breath, nausea, fatigue and other symptoms. New rules to limit these dangerous volatile organic compounds (VOCs) inside cars are being introduced around the world.

Paint is another example of a familiar smell that says 'new, clean and fresh' when the true sound should be alarm bells. I first took notice when the woman running the pre-natal classes we attended before our first child nonchalantly told us that we'd need to finish painting the nursery three months before the baby's due date. It seemed a given to the clearly better prepared parents-to-be in the group, who nodded sagely and carried on studying the pros and cons of epidurals, but I'd never heard that advice before. I spent the rest of the session madly jabbing at my phone trying to work out why paint was so awful there had to be a 90-day moratorium before the air inside our home was considered safe for new lungs, eyes and skin. It was those VOCs again.

We spend so much time and effort trying to mitigate our effect on the world out there that we forget 'the environment' doesn't stop at our threshold. The USA's Environmental Protection Agency states that concentrations of many VOCs are up to ten times higher indoors than they are outdoors thanks to thousands of products that are regularly used in our homes without us even registering them or their smell.[16]

It lists paints, cleansers and disinfectants, air fresheners, pesticides, solvents, wood preservatives, aerosol sprays, even dry-cleaned clothing.

Manufacturers can legally claim their products are safe, despite the VOCs, because each individual item only produces, let's say, one hundredth of a toxic dose. They somehow forget, as seemingly do industry regulators, that we are never exposed to just one at a time.

Thanks to that prenatal class, we had invested in an admittedly expensive VOC-free paint from a UK manufacturer to slap on the walls when we moved house a few years ago.

Needless to say, there hasn't been a can of air freshener or a paraffin-based scented candle (so bad for us the UK government is on the brink of banning them) for some time. And we hadn't done a dry cleaning run since we'd tried and failed to convince the puzzled proprietor on our high street that we didn't want to get our clothes back in plastic sleeves.

By then, something was dawning on us. If some of our every-day cleaning cupboard staples were dangerous, we needed to look with some urgency at the everyday lotions, potions, and cleaners we were putting on our skin or sluicing down the drain. Zero waste had already done us a massive unacknowledged favour on that front. When we stopped buying food wrapped in plastic out too went the big brand cleaning products, from fabric detergent to floor cleaner and dishwasher tablets. At the same time that we learned new recipes for food we had to do the same for cleaning solutions – before our own aroma became socially unacceptable.

Solid bars were an easy swap for cleaning ourselves and some aspects of our home – though it turns out you still have to be a little wary of the ingredients – and the children have great fun making bath bombs and fizzing toilet cleaners from safe cupboard essentials.

A wooden brush and a dish of soap rather than a bottle of Fairy now sit on our kitchen sink. Unfortunately, guests never offer to do the washing up because they're not quite sure what to do with them.

But somewhere in our collective memory we do all still remember the days before commercially produced cleaners. We know, for example, that a good way of cleaning windows to that all-important streak-free gleam is to use vinegar and newspaper.

Homemade cleaning products rely heavily on vinegar, as well as bicarbonate of soda, citric acid, water and, if you're feeling decadent, some essential oil. Unsurprisingly, our house smelled like a chip shop for a while.

So we adjusted the ratios, acknowledged the importance of distilled white vinegar rather than whatever we could plunder from the kitchen shelves, steeped that vinegar in leftover citrus peel and finally started to get somewhere. Our floors were clean, our bathrooms smelled of oranges and the kids could safely rummage around in the kitchen without the risk of drinking the bleach or rinse aid for whatever reason kids do life-threatening things when you least expect it.

Meanwhile, bicarb works in the dishwasher too. And I do so love our dishwasher. Third hand, even this ancient article uses far less water to work through a round of dishes, pots, pans and cutlery than washing by hand. When you've had a day in which even the smallest of green decisions felt like hard work, knowing you're making a better choice simply by pressing the on button and walking away is sometimes the best feeling in the world.

We had even found a work around for the seemingly impossible task of finding a toilet brush whose bristles, handle and/or holder weren't made of plastic. They are now far more common – just watch out for nylon bristles that break off and get flushed away – but after a year of looking we had few options but to concoct our own holder from a metal florist's bucket. It's a talking point, at least.

So then we had to tackle the beast that was the clothes wash. Despite having the most stain-attracting children in the world, we'd already stopped buying laundry stain remover years earlier after a few of their items that had been left soaking a little too long got chemical burn marks and holes. That stuff wasn't going near my kids' skin again for all the whitest of whites in the playground.

We found lemon juice, vinegar, grated soap and even just prompt rinsing cleared up most stains, and barely a summer's day goes by that I'm not whipping would-be whites into the sun's rays in a bid to brighten them up. Who knew milk could get rid of ink stains?

But how on earth do you get through a loadful of everyday clothes without a family-sized box of something well branded and familiarly fragrant?

We trawled the web and came up with soap nuts, which seem highly unlikely when they arrive with their little mesh bag to fling happily into the washing machine. I won't tell you what they remind me of as this isn't that kind of book, but those shrivelled fruit shells contain saponin, a natural surfactant that works with water to separate the grime from cloth by reducing the water's surface tension in much the same way that synthetic options do. They are also easy to grow organically. Once they've been shown the cycle several times over, the compost bin calls.

The only drawback is that the trees are grown thousands of miles away in places like Taiwan, Nepal and India. So David did a bit more digging and came up, I kid you not, with conkers, not least because he remembers seeing bubbles forming on the surface of puddles where cars had run over the best endeavours of the big horse chestnut tree on his school route. Smash up conkers, immerse them in hot water for a while and they apparently release that same saponin as soap nuts. I checked. There really were bubbles.

I was still sceptical though, a situation that was not improved by the sight of David sitting legs akimbo on the sitting room carpet one autumn evening with a hammer in one hand, one of these beautiful childhood weapons in the other and an eye on *Countryfile*. Several chunks were lost under the sofa never to be seen again as he stoically worked his way through an auburn pile. It's a lot of faff, though, and life really is too short to spend your evenings bashing conkers to bits.

It's probably not worth holding out hope that they'll mimic a traditional detergent with its softeners, whiteners and fragrances. But we're prepared to swap out the box with irritation warnings

We need to talk about water

We tend to assume that treatment plants will save us from our watery sins. Perhaps we're confident the wet wipes or sanitary products flushed down the loo will get fished out long before they hit open water or we're convinced there must be some clever neutralising solution that magically turns a harmful soup into crystal clear H2O.

But the truth is that a chemical cocktail arising from 'business as usual' lifestyles is wreaking havoc in streams, rivers, ponds and lakes.

Phosphates sprayed onto crops and added to our laundry and dishwasher detergents leach into waterways, where they have the same fertilising effect. They make algae bloom, sapping the oxygen from the water and suffocating the life around it.

Meanwhile, the synthetic surfactants found in many of our under-the-sink stashes reduce water tension to allow easy absorption of other pollutants by animals and plants.

Yet more of the compounds we swirl down the plughole are so toxic to wildlife that they disrupt the hormones in mammals and fish – an impact that was starting to sound more and more familiar.

There's a weird blindness to our water pollution. We happily trot out the old good news story that the river Thames is now so clean that it is home to otters. Indeed, the briefest glimpse of otter sighting records in the Thames Valley would suggest we're all going in the right direction.[33]

The wider reality however, is that the UK's waterways are mired in muck. Every single river in England is currently failing the Environment Agency's test for pollution and only 14% are of a good ecological standard due to the sheer quantity of sewage, agricultural and industrial chemicals flooding, pouring or seeping into them. In other words there isn't a single river around here in a good place.

And it is getting worse fast. Water companies' pollution track record is now angrily branded 'unacceptable' by central government as well as by campaigners, residents' groups and affected businesses.

The Environment Agency revealed more than 400,000 incidents of dumping raw sewage into the UK's waterways in 2020. Independent calculations suggest that meant raw sewage was pumped into UK rivers for more than 3.1 million hours over the course of the year.

And yet, in October 2021, days before hosting the UN Climate Change Conference known better as Cop26, the UK government, including our own MP, voted against amendments to the Environment Bill that included placing a legal requirement on water companies to reduce raw sewage discharges into UK rivers. The public outcry forced a partial U-turn.

and signs depicting dead fish for fewer, natural surfactants and a bit more elbow grease.

Plus soap nuts, conkers and, to be fair, plain old water do shift some dirt – at least to the extent that we still have some conkers for emergencies. We make a point of only collecting the conkers we really need and planting up several each year because the horse chestnut tree is now vulnerable to extinction.

Our clean laundry now smells… neutral. In fact, after a while we started coming up against a weird new problem. The opposite of nose-blind, the removal of strong smelling products from our everyday life meant that when we came across them elsewhere they hit us like a freight train.

I even started booking haircuts for first thing in the morning in a bid to avoid the build up of that salon smell that I never used to register but now makes my head ache and my stomach turn over.

I admit I still struggle with the lack of scent a bit though. All those learned social behaviours and implied associations around cleanliness and being organised enough to be demonstrably on top of the washing pile, all the while smelling of something alluring and luxuriant and somehow successful, are all things I miss a little.

At the school gates, when the children's friends leave the 'just washed' smell in their wake and their polo shirts dazzle in the morning light, I'm still a tiny bit jealous.

When I last commented on a friend's lovely new perfume as we hugged she leaned back, looked at me and said 'You smell of… nothing.' I should really take that as the mere statement of fact it was meant to be. One day I hope I'll be able to. But I'm also not stocking up on *eau de toilette* anytime soon either.

I was roundly cursing the day I ditched A level chemistry by this point, wishing I could tell my 16-year-old self not to swap to ancient history because understanding the risks of crossing the Rubicon in

Dirty cosmetics

Like lots of people, I'd occasionally had a go at pronouncing the list of complex long-winded ingredients on the back of a shampoo bottle. I usually managed a line, absolute maximum, before the consonants started swimming among the bubbles.

One of those ingredients in your typical bottle is Sodium Lauryl Sulfate or Sulphate, depending on where you or the bottle are in the world. It is also known as sodium dodecyl sulphate, though you might also find it listed as sodium monolauryl sulphate, sodium salt, hydrogen sulphate or sodium dodecanesulphate.

Sodium Lauryl Sulfate is an irritant. Sometimes it acts as a detergent. Sometimes it is a surfactant that makes the bubbles in shampoo, toothpaste, body wash, hand wash and some soap, as well as laundry and cleaning products. It is still used to degrease car engines – the purpose it was originally created for back in the early 20th Century.

Sodium Lauryl Sulfate is commonly derived from either coconut or palm oil, so along with the plastic bottle and the fact that, particularly in its raw form, SLS is 'moderately toxic to aquatic life'[34] it's a no-no in our house – even if it can technically and regularly is included in products labelled '100% natural' by the nearest greenwasher.

Then there are parabens, which extend the shelf life of a wide range of products because they prevent the growth of bacteria and fungi. You'll find them in moisturisers, suncream, deodorants, toothpaste, make-up, cleansers and many other staples. Absorbed through the skin and used since the 1920s there are serious concerns about the effect of parabens on both human and environmental health because they are hormone disruptors.

Widely used in four different forms, and subject to different restrictions by different countries, the EU banned two parabens in 2015 because of health concerns. By 2017, the UN Environment Programme had labelled the lot 'endocrine-disrupting

Beware parabens Cottonbro, Pexels

chemicals.' Even at low levels at least one type of paraben kills coral and all have that same hormone-disrupting potential in aquatic life.

Phthalates are used to make plastic flexible and difficult to break, and can also act as a binding agent. You find them in nail polish, hairspray, and shampoo (again). They are also present in a huge range of household items including but not limited to vinyl flooring, some wallpapers, raincoats, shower curtains and food packaging where they are suspected of leaching into food. The EU and several other authorities in Canada and the USA have been gradually tightening their grip on phthalates for several years now. They also seem to carry an endocrine risk, though there is little research to go on for the moment. It is highly likely phthalates are present in all our bodies, especially those of young children and childbearing-aged women.[36]

Those trying to avoid exposure to phthalates tend to avoid anything with fragrance or perfume.

49 BC wasn't going to be nearly as handy when buying moisturiser.

I nor anyone else I know has the time to pick through the endless lists of unpronounceables or greenwashing spin designed to deflect our attention from what is in our benign-looking lotions and potions. Once again the easiest, cheapest, most reassuring solution we could come up with (as real people with real lives) was to cut them out entirely and move on.

Shampoo and soap bars whose five item ingredients lists read reassuringly like a pantry inventory from back in the day were already gracing our sinks and showers thanks to our stance on plastic. A few earlier purchasing swaps miraculously also adhered to the newly added 'no-nasties' criteria, but the bathroom was looking bare. I started looking into homemade cosmetics, picking out the options from authoritative sources whose list of ingredients I recognised, could pronounce and had a chance of finding in our kitchen.

We don't have sensitive skin in general, though the patch test is still sacrosanct and we always sense check the use of ingredients against expert advice before concocting anything. But food-grade oil, oats, honey, some contact-safe essential oils, apple cider vinegar (which we'd made by accident the previous year) and cucumber have all helped to make moisturiser, toners and the like.

The kids think raiding the salad drawer for a beauty treatment is the funniest thing they've ever heard of but there are certainly plenty of people out there who still know how to use genuinely natural ingredients for their everyday needs.

Again it struck us that a whisper of knowledge is still there – just under the surface of our collective consciousness. Honey surprises nobody as an antibiotic marvel and who hasn't at least once thanked their lucky stars for aloe vera to soothe bad sunburn? How about those millions of teenagers fervently praying the acne outbreak will subside while reaching for the tea tree?

Speaking of whom I was by now busy channelling my awkward 14-year-old self. I was Youtubing how-to tutorials in a bid to get to grips with a whole new world of eco friendly, no plastic, no nasties, mostly powder make-up.

It hadn't started well. Despite trawling the web for weeks on the hunt for new ways to decorate my face while ticking each box on an ever growing list of eco musts, my first buy resulted in an exciting little parcel of powders in tins and cardboard tubes of lipsticks postmarked... Australia. They literally could not have come from further away. They may have even been air freighted, I didn't dare look. And then my son found them, opened the lot and used them all to 'paint pictures with.'

It came at just the wrong time for my self confidence. The loss of those tiny and yet startlingly expensive metal pots I'd been saving for a special occasion – as visually and ergonomically appealing to me as they were to my son – hit me stupidly hard.

I had already swapped my disposable razor for a metal one, swallowing the fear I would immediately open an artery, if only when changing the blades. It turned out to be as easy as using a disposable version, which was a surprise to me – the twit who hadn't clocked the fact that the plastic throwaways are based on the original design.

And when I first unpacked a menstrual cup from its unbleached cardboard box David took one look, declared it 'a hell of a commitment to the cause' and exited as if pursued by a bear. I'll never go back to throwaways though, not least because I won't ever again have to traipse around unfamiliar streets at some antisocial hour looking for a supermarket or pharmacy or just a pub vending machine when caught uncomfortably short. That in itself is worth the swap any month of any year.

These days, our deodorant comes from its manufacturer on the Isle of Wight in a cardboard tube and solid form sunscreen (think cricketers' war paint) arrives in the same form. Even toothpaste is scooped from a glass jar. The only thing that we unquestionably accept in traditional form is medication.

And because of the now familiar layered criteria effect, plenty of other beauty 'essentials' had fallen by the wayside too including almost every anti-ageing item out there and hair dye just as the greys really started to make their presence felt. Even my regular disposable contact lens order – little plastic semi circles wrapped in individual hard plastic cases – had long been ditched in favour of glasses.

David, your typical low maintenance male whose only concession to grooming was his hair clippers and now – big news – a stainless steel toothbrush with a wooden replaceable head, hadn't seen a great change in his ablutions.

Gradually the once limited choices out there started to multiply and became real, reliable and affordable options that were gaining traction. Suddenly I wasn't the only person whose toothbrush was bamboo or whose make up pads were reusable.

I was delighted to see the brand of unbleached recycled bamboo toilet roll that arrives at our house in brightly coloured paper[17] every few months also pop up at our local pub. If there's an antidote to feeling cosmetically isolated, it's validation from the local boozer.

It was also good to know we were no longer contributing to the fatbergs that now seem a permanent feature in modern life – whether they are deep down in London sewers or rotting on South Coast beaches.

When our youngest child came along we had a ridiculously late-in-the-day epiphany of the reusable nappy variety. Our parents had used them on us, but we had only ever reached for the disposable option until we called time on our bin. Then we prepared to embrace what we feared would be a world of stinking pails and stabbing the baby or ourselves with gigantic safety pins.

It turns out the brave new world of reusable nappies is, these days, one of designer prints, idiot-proof all-in-one construction and, thank god, poppers. We bought a bundle of just twelve nappies second-hand that were each designed to work from newborn to toddler and went for it. The throwaway wet wipes were replaced with cotton muslins and an existing flask of water.

The lot cost us the same as a month's supply of the disposable variety and when our son obliged us by potty training at record speed we managed to resell them on for the price we had paid. It was a definitive win-win. There had admittedly been a few leakages while we got to grips with absorption but the whole experience, including the curious enquiries from other parents and nursery staff was, unexpectedly, just the boost we needed.

For a moment, somewhere in the middle of 2018 we felt like we had done quite a deep dive into another critical aspect of sustainability and come up with some good, workable and sometimes even easy solutions. We even had the sneaking suspicion that we'd done our health another massive favour, too.

And then, yet again, the hole we'd picked in the corner of an issue started to unravel away from us in a way that we were starting, uneasily, to recognise as part of the process.

The common criticism with cloth nappies is that they use a lot of very hot water to wash. That's true, though it turns out that when washed at 60°, line-dried in a large load and eventually passed on to another child, they come in at around 60g of CO_2e per nappy compared with 130g CO_2e for a disposable or the 165g CO_2e spent on a reusable boiled at 90° in each wash before being tumble-dried.[18]

Clearly, though, it was time to address the next problem. That while we had acknowledged the importance of what was in the water we sent down the drain, quantity was another matter.

Water feels like the ultimate closed cycle. The school textbook diagram of rain falling on mountains and returning to the sea to be sucked up again, is reassuring in every way. Besides, we're an island nation with a soggy maritime climate, there's water everywhere. Conserving the stuff was low on our priority list to be honest. But it should have been far higher, far earlier.

The world may be more than 70% water, but only 1% of that is accessible and suitable for consumption. More than two thirds of that feeds and waters domestically managed animals, leaving precious little for all other life, including our own.

In the UK, we're pretty vague about water. We believe we use less than 20 litres a day. In fact, it is 142 litres per day – more than in most other European countries.[19] We see what we wrongly think is extensive rainfall, watch water pouring from leaking pipes unheeded by water companies and dismiss this as a non-problem. We certainly did in our house. But with the UK population alone set to exceed 70 million people by the end of the decade[20] at the same time that climate change is making its presence felt, Britain is now at real risk of running out of water.

'Unless we take action to change things, we will not have enough water to supply our needs.' So said James Bevan, chief executive of the Environment Agency, in a radio interview about the situation in the UK in 20-25 years. 'We need water wastage to be as socially unacceptable as blowing smoke in the face of a baby.' I remember that interview. The frustration in his voice and the starkness of the image made me and, I'm sure, plenty of others sit up and take notice for the first time.

These days, like millions of other people, we collect our rainwater from the roof to distribute around the garden, we have showers not baths, there are bricks in the cisterns, we religiously turn the tap off while brushing teeth and lathering hands and bodies, and the kids get extra pocket money if they clean the car (only done on very special occasions) within three buckets of water and no hose pipe.

When you turn a tap in our house, the expectation is that you'll turn it just enough to release a trickle rather than a tidal wave, though we're still on the hunt for tap aerators that fit our antiquated fixtures.

If we need to clean vegetables, we don't hold them under constantly running water, they get plunged into a single bowlful that is then emptied either straight onto the garden or into the water butt outside, as does any drained, cooled cooking water.

We all have stainless steel water canteens – a hangover from travelling a few years ago. Using those means we don't have endless cups of half drunk water everywhere and we know how hydrated the children are as a welcome bonus. If cups or glasses are used, the remainder goes straight into plant pots.

Our son, now a four-year-old water play aficionado does play a little fast and loose with this most mesmerising of substances and I'm not yet fully on board with the whole 'If it's yellow let it mellow…' mantra. I'm trying, though.

Water made us start to realise that we need to see everything – absolutely everything – as a valuable resource. When we're finished using something, the first thought needs to be: 'What else can I use this for?' That has to start with something as seemingly infinite, omnipresent and therefore unimportant – for those that have it at least – as water.

The aim, every day, is that as little as possible goes down the drain and then only once it has been used as many times as possible.

We're still finding new ways to save water but this is one of the few changes that does have a measurable effect. Last year our water bill dropped by more than £200 on top of savings from previous years. Most of that was probably because we resurrected the spot clean and the sniff test.

Ours is a nation that brags about how often the washing machine goes on every week. If the kids' uniforms are freshly laundered every day you must be winning in life. Aside from the water and energy and time involved in cleaning things when they just don't need it, there's something resolutely 1950s housewife about all this that rankles more than a little. And yet, as with that 'just washed' smell and all its unspoken social signposting, I found it surprisingly tough to disengage from those habits.

Indulgent navel gazing wasn't going to get us or our water usage anywhere fast though and we had soon switched from shoving clothes into the washing machine simply because it was the end of the day to washing things only when they were actually dirty.

This attitude shift wasn't revolutionary but it was a bit of a milestone, and alongside saving us a lot of water, adopting a real world approach to washing our clothes gave us back a lot more than clean undies.

5. Wardrobe Malfunction

Shaking ourselves out of that blindness to water finally forced us to square up to a hidden plastic that even a year and a half after Beanbag Day was still slipping past us in plain sight.

We had long had a sense of disquiet about the contents of our clothing. When we finally tackled it, it was eye-opening. And not in a good way.

❇ ❇ ❇

The biggest problem is that microplastics in synthetic fabrics are lighter than air. Behaving like dust, small particles can be inhaled by humans. Most will be purged by our body's mucus clearance mechanisms, but some could stay where they may cause inflammation, especially in people who struggle to clear their respiratory system.[21]

Scientists are also concerned that contaminants hitching a ride on fibrous microplastics could cause damage to genetic information within cells. Some experts are looking at how the plastic itself along with its additives, such as dye, could disrupt the reproductive system, change genetic material and promote cancer.[22]

I really thought ditching plastics would be one of those easy wins, that it would only be a few months before we happily saw the back of them all. That was almost four years ago. But, just like their hard plastic peers, these objects are still scarily difficult to remove from family life.

David is a keen amateur sportsman so he has 'kit' coming out of his ears and – more of an issue – the kids are into dressing up in a big way. We haven't bought any of those outfits that now line supermarket aisles at Christmas, Halloween and everything in between for years, but thanks to hand-me-down bundles and well meaning gifts they just seem to appear.

Then there are the fabrics that don't even register – the army of soft toys, the cushions and their covers, the sofa I was so proud to have rescued from a skip. And what about our duvets? Are they throwing up synthetic dust every time we turn over in bed? And just how worried about that should we be?

I was struggling to find out, wading yet again through complicated academic papers. The approach, as usual, should have been that we used the resources and products that are in our home for as long as possible before we gave away, recycled or repurposed them. But by now I was pretty uneasy about these materials hanging around, especially the kids' sleeping arrangements under duvets we'd only ever really thought about when we put a cover on them.

We saved up and bought them wool duvets from a manufacturer that creates them from that undervalued commodity, British wool, in a factory 50 miles from our home. They're expensive – so we're staggering the adults' upgrade – but the savings we make elsewhere by going zero softened the blow.

We couldn't perform the usual blanket ban on all items coming in through the front door for one reason – the children's synthetic school uniform. The original decision on materials by the school had been made for partly environmental reasons, too – half of it is made from post consumer recycled plastic.

That is a good thing. Recycled plastic in its various forms is used in a thousand different ways – from park benches and car interiors to rugs and cushions. In other words it is a commodity – something worth hanging on to, keeping back rather than burning it or dumping into the wider environment, and even gathering back up once it has been discarded.

This value circle – one that, along with the eco credentials boost, really does seem to make sense to a business's bottom line – is a key part of the fight to reduce our plastic impact on the planet.

But while we will, when a genuine need arises, buy second-hand items made from hard form recycled plastic, we won't buy any more synthetic material no matter what the origin of that material – because of those damned breakaways.

Meanwhile, deciding what was coming into our home didn't help sort out what we were going to do with the material already there. And that was turning into a bit of a headache.

If there has ever been something in our home we no longer need but is still of value and use, the next step, as in many households, has been to sell it or give it away. We could have done the same thing here. We could have boxed these clothes and soft furnishings up – though we would probably have had to extract the much loved dressing up stuff in the dead of night – and passed them on.

But by the time we were grappling with this aspect of the journey towards zero, the limits of those responsibilities were starting to look a little indistinct.

So we invested in a Guppy washing bag designed to trap the fibrous microplastics breaking away from clothing while being pummelled in the machine. We use it to wash anything with a synthetic component.

Spinning it out

Soft but durable, quick drying, wrinkle-free, colour fast, resistant to wear, tear and unravelling, synthetic fibres have been received with such enthusiasm that there were 'riots' over nylon when it was rereleased in the USA after the Second World War.

Anna Khomutova, Pexels

Joined by an array of equally miraculous plastic fibres by the middle of the last century, this one type of synthetic fibre, first designed in the 1930s by an army of Dupont scientists, is now found in hundreds of products ranging from scrubbing brushes and kites to shoes and tights.

Synthetic materials shouldn't be confused with regenerated fibres made from cellulose polymers found in plants such as cotton or wood pulp. Viscose, acetate, triacetate, rayon and now new types of rayon known as modal and lyocell (or the brand name Tencel) are all regenerated fibres.

But if your label refers to polyester, acrylic, nylon, elastane, Lycra or spandex, polyolefin or polyamide it's essentially plastic – sourced from coal and oil and refined into monomers that are then joined together into seemingly infinite lengths, in a process called polymerisation. And don't forget the blended materials such as polycottons – part cotton and part polyester.

Around 60 million metric tonnes of plastic textile fibres are produced every year. Rising by around 6% a year, that means the poster boy of the plastic world might be the water bottle or the plastic bag, but at 16% of the world's total plastic production[37] that benign looking synthetic top or even the kids' teddies should be right up there too.

The problem is the breakdown of those plastic fibres produce tiny microplastics, some of which have the potential to travel thousands of miles just like natural dust. Remember the microplastic soup under the Great Pacific garbage patch and the microplastic snow falling on the seemingly pristine Pyrenees? That's the stuff – sloughing off textile-like plastics as well as disintegrating from the hard items we are somehow more tuned into.

As I write, scientists are now finding microplastics in snow near the summit of Everest, alongside long-standing evidence of these nasty little specimens at the bottom of the Mariana Trench in the western Pacific Ocean. They are literally everywhere.

Your average washing machine cycle is the perfect combination of abrasion, heat and chemical exposure via detergents to accelerate the breakdown of materials. In fact a delicates wash – which typically uses twice as much water as a normal cycle – releases an average of 800,000 microplastic fibres.

Calculations by the University of California suggest that every 100,000 people produce more than a kilogram of microplastics every single day, just from doing their laundry. As a result of something as automatic, unconscious and everyday as the process of washing our clothes, the UK flushes enough microplastics down the drain every year to make 49 million plastic bags.

Globally since the 1950s, we have produced 5.6 million tonnes of synthetic microfibres just from washing our clothes. The really scary thing is that half of it has happened in the past ten years.

With no factory-fitted filter on our washing machine, the Guppy was our only line of defence until we made our own from a bucket and an ultra fine mesh made from an old washing bag that had sprung a hole. Filters are an easy win and we can't really understand why manufacturers still haven't been obliged by law to fit them before new washing machines roll off the production line.

Several manufacturers are now pushing designs that protect fibres by minimising drum rotation and friction. But at the time of writing, only Beko has introduced a microplastics filter to its new appliances in the UK which, it claims, removes 90% of microplastics from waste water.

The UK government has been infuriatingly slow to tackle this massive aspect of plastic pollution. As things stand it merely promises to work with clothing manufacturers to make more sustainable choices, and with the water industry to address the issue of microplastics in wastewater.

While we take significant measures to reduce the release of microplastic fibres into the water system, we know we're in the minority at the moment. In other words, we know that if we did send the synthetic materials to the charity shop on the high street, our actions would indirectly increase plastic pollution at sea and on land. We literally couldn't stomach that.

The pressure we were starting to put on ourselves was becoming a bit intense to say the least. But we sure as hell weren't about to give up and bin it all now.

Three quarters of UK consumers throw away clothes they no longer want or need, rather than recycling them or even donating them to charity, because, they claim, they didn't realise they could. The bin is the default.

Scale that up and the global numbers are breathtaking – a bin lorry's worth of clothes is tipped into landfill or burned every single second of every single day.

But the tide is turning and it may, bizarrely, be due to changes in behaviour as a result of Covid-19. Since the UK's first 'proper' pandemic lockdown in spring 2020, a quarter of us now say we repair our clothes. One in five say we keep items for longer. More than 10% of British consumers now buy second-hand or vintage clothing and others look for sustainable textiles. We're with them all the way because for us, this has been yet another one of those win-win consumption resets.

Putting downward pressure on our water consumption means our clothes don't go through the tortures of the drum nearly as often. The garments last longer, look better and we don't spend money replacing them as often.

There's also the 'don't wash it at all' strategy. It may sound grim, but it really can work. No wash clubs that encourage you to air out and spot clean clothes – especially jeans – are a thing. Converts save water, detergent and dramatically reduce the wear and tear on clothes, helping them last far longer. As I write, the jeans I all but live in haven't seen the inside of a washing machine for four months.

With so much about the denim production process causing catastrophic environmental damage, particularly around water use and dye pollution in some of the poorest and least regulated parts of the world, that is a double-win.

Try it. I dare you. Just remember the airing bit is key – ideally by an open window.

Extending the active life of our clothes from an average of 2.2 years by just nine months would reduce their water, waste and carbon dioxide footprint by up to 30%. Since I've got T-shirts that I've had for 20 years, I thought this would be easy.

But long-life clothes were only part of the problem. It turns out that every tonne of clothing that is kept out of landfill and directly re-used – either because it is sold or given away – could mean a net carbon dioxide gas reduction of 11 tonnes thanks to savings from production right the way through to disposal.

So with a *modus operandi* now emerging, we decided on the next immediately effective blanket ban – new clothes. No matter the work-wear, school wear, last minute purchase because a child had vomited down you, even footwear, it should be sourced second-hand.

That surely wasn't going to be a big deal, we had plenty to see us through and anyway, we were tight on disposable cash at the time and the diary was reassuringly free of big social events. We had some time to get ourselves into the swing of this.

But within a week we'd been invited to a wedding, a posh 50th birthday party and somehow I'd received an invite to the BAFTA film and TV awards. What the hell was I going to wear?

I had nothing that would come close to an appropriate outfit, the second-hand shops around us were not that way inclined and my friends are all taller and slimmer. Then one of them suggested hiring something. At no point did I imagine that going zero would involve opening the door to the postie holding three enormous boxes like she was playing a cameo in *Breakfast at Tiffany's*.

We'd learned that eco meant less, smaller, simpler and, dare I say it, a bit more beige. But opening those boxes on the hallway floor because I couldn't wait long enough to make it to the sofa was an experience in luxury and colour and dresses wrapped in tissue paper that I will never forget. I wanted to throw something shiny and fluttery in the air exuberantly.

I'd selected three designer 'pieces' from an occasion wear hire company called Girl Meets Dress to try on, pick from and return a couple of days later. Even the boxes and internal packaging were reused and recycled and yes, their cleaning processes stood up to inspection too. The total bill, incredibly, was just £45.

This was permissive, expansive, fun and a great deal cheaper. It couldn't have been better timed – a bit of guilt-free light relief just when we had hit a bit of a brick wall of complexity, confusion, frustration, and few clear solutions elsewhere in the going zero process.

I stood there twirling in a posh frock and mismatching socks, convinced I was dodging some sort of universal rule, muttering like an idiot: 'you shall go to the ball.' Even if it did take several minutes to wrestle the box onto the overhead rack in front of an audience on the train the following day, it was worth it.

The event itself was one of those dreamlike experiences with celeb faces at every turn – one that I knew I would never forget and certainly never repeat in my life, but it didn't matter. This was champagne on a lemonade budget. I reckon Audrey would have approved.

I had been lucky to have found something 'vintage' in my size made from natural fibres that I loved wearing before boxing it all back up and waving it goodbye ready for the next Hepburn.

From then on we would definitely be wearing someone else's clothes on important days – hopefully with the same childlike glee. For the first time in ages we had found a solution where the feelgood factor came first.

Dressing for real life was somewhat trickier, however, not least because – although we knew the materials to avoid – we were really unsure about the ones to look for on those second hand labels.

We started reading up on the production of yet more of the products and materials we had always taken for granted.

Take cotton. Even if the product is biodegradable at the end of its life, 10,000 litres of water is used to make one kilo – equivalent to a single pair of jeans and a T-shirt. I did a bit of number crunching and it turns out that amount of fluid would sustain a person for seven and a half years. Such demand means entire rivers are diverted to satisfy it, with huge effects on downstream ecosystems, from Australia to India.

The true cost of fast fashion

Plenty has been said about the way we treat our clothing and the effect of our fashion decisions on the planet. But the truth is that our careful considerations can go out of the window when faced with a tight budget and a pair of jeans £30 cheaper than the others, let alone articles like a now infamous garment that sold on Black Friday for just 8p.

I'm no psychologist but this is surely not the way to imply fundamental value in the physical resources or human effort involved. And it is certainly no indicator of environmental cost.

The latest data suggests the fashion and clothing industry is now responsible for between 8 and 10% of global CO2e emissions – dwarfing the aviation industry, for example, which was responsible for around 2.4% of global CO2e emissions from fossil fuels in 2018.

Human demand for new clothing consumes 79 trillion litres of water a year and causes 20% of global industrial water pollution.

Even before we decide a particular shade or cut isn't for us and leave it on the hanger or drop it in the bin, 92 million tonnes of waste textiles have already been created and cast aside to satisfy a demand for new clothes that has doubled since 2000.[38] Doubled since Millennium Eve.

In the UK alone, we chuck £140 million worth of the clothes we have ended up with into landfill every single year – more than any other European country.

Buying items before returning them is only adding to the problem, with one study in 2018 reporting that businesses worldwide were dumping more than 2.2 million tonnes of returns because they didn't have the systems in place to process the returned items.

These are all massive numbers but they suggest one thing – that we simply fail to appreciate our clothing. In fact, despite a surge in the volume of clothes and shoes we own, our spending on them dropped from around 30% of disposable income in the 1950s to 12% by 2009. In 2020, it fell to 5%.

In the USA, the average consumer now purchases an item of clothing every five days. British shoppers are not far behind.

Karolina Grabowska, Pexels

Even if that battery of figures dazzles you – as it did me – the idea that it is completely normal to buy clothes that often should light up a big flashing sign in our heads that reads: 'This is broken.'

Meanwhile, cotton is the most chemically sprayed crop on the planet. Accounting for a sixth of all pesticide use in the world, it threatens people and wildlife in the immediate vicinity and for miles around thanks to run off. So if we want a cotton T-shirt it needs to tick the recycled box and, preferably, the organic one too before it even comes off the second-hand hanger.

On the other hand, linen – sourced from the flax plant – is considerably less thirsty as long as it is grown closer to home in its natural Northern Europe habitat. It is also pretty resilient, making it slower to wear out. Regularly grown without chemical intervention, where flax does get sprayed, it demands a lot less than other crops. Plus, every part of the plant is used, including the root, which is left in the soil to act as a fertiliser, reinvigorating the soil. Flax even retains almost four tonnes of C02e per hectare a year.

Sadly, though, flax has been crowded out by decades of accumulated cheap synthetic fibres and hybrid mixes, leaving little to be found in our local charity or vintage shops or even online. Nor, for that matter, is there an abundance of other natural fibre garments and there's still no sign of regenerated materials at all. I look forward to the day that changes.

❃ ❃ ❃

Shopping for the simplest garment now involves a mental checklist: is it a natural or regenerated material? Is it organically produced? Is it made in the UK? Is it second-hand? Only then do we get to the question of whether we like it very much or even if it's in the right size.

As you'll have guessed, very few things make it through that checklist. Which is fine when time is on your side and you can come back and trawl through the rails another day. Then it feels measured and calm and positive.

But we all know sometimes you need something to wear sharpish.

The fact that 2020's Covid lockdown was spent largely in a heatwave was good for many reasons. For me it was crucial. I had ripped my jeans in a way that wasn't fixable – at least not by my unskilled hands – and having had a particularly vicious, and in hindsight, badly timed wardrobe clear out, I was down to a single pair of shorts. Had it been chilly I'd have been in big trouble. Either way I was stuck.

The second-hand shops on our high street were firmly closed and I couldn't guarantee that anything I bought online wouldn't come in a plastic post bag, regardless of the fact that we ask for reused, non-plastic packaging every time we make an e-purchase.

I was a grown woman with a happy, healthy family and a success-ful career, sitting in my own home and yet the severe, self-imposed purchasing rules we'd made up meant I didn't own a single pair of wearable trousers and now couldn't go out and buy one either.

We'd trapped ourselves in some weird purchasing prison and for what? I just needed a pair of jeans like the rest of the world. This was ridiculous.

If ever there was a time to loosen up a bit, to give ourselves a break, to buy whatever we wanted, to indulge in a bit of retail thera-py like we used to – and like the rest of the neighbours were happily doing judging by the delivery vans – the height of a global pandem-ic was surely that time.

Instead, I just waited, hoped the increasingly battered shorts wouldn't fall apart before the R number came down and, like every-one else, made sure my Zoom calls were broadcast from the waist up.

We have never been great followers of fashion and we didn't ever worry unduly that going zero would restrict our self expres-sion. But even we could see that having personal preference appear so far down the purchasing pecking order could impact how we presented ourselves to the world, perhaps even how we felt about ourselves and our identities.

Don't get me wrong, on the grand scale of things, giving your-self permission to whimsically buy a top that happens to catch your eye is low on the list compared with not poisoning the planet, but when we decided to see if we could take it up a gear, the choices got tighter still.

We had come a long way. Yet again, our purchasing decisions were unrecognisable from those we would have made just a cou-ple of years earlier. But it's one thing to buy, say, an organic cotton T-shirt whose brand also turns a profit from unethically mass-pro-duced synthetics. It's another to ensure that everyday purchase feeds profits back into a business whose ethics align with your own.

Online auction sites are full of luxury and high end high street brands that recoup some cash for those who are finished with them. Back when we had picked and chosen from the whole world and its fashions pre Beanbag Day, I always used to have one part of my brain calculating resale values when I bought 'nice' clothes – especially for the kids. I certainly wasn't the only one.

Perhaps if we could – in some microscopic way – help create demand for sustainable brands and materials when sold on, we could help influence other people who did buy new to plump for sustainable brands because they knew they might get a few quid back later on.

Could we do just a tiny bit more to help change the trajectory of an industry that comes only behind housing, transport and food in its environmental impact? Could we wring out one more squeeze? Could we strip this all back one more step so our second-hand clothes and footwear not only fit the now quite long list of must haves (or, more likely, have nots) but also originated only from brands that were environmental forces for good as a whole?

No. It turned out we couldn't.

We don't buy many clothes as a family but even with our low level requirements, we just couldn't find the items we needed if we stuck to such a restrictive list. With the focus on sustainable fashion only now coming through – however loudly – into the mainstream high street, there simply isn't the volume of second-hand items trickling through to edit that far, to reduce the impact of our clothing consumption quite that much. Yet.

We have always said that this whole sustainable adventure is a journey, that we would screw things up, go a bit far and find ourselves backtracking – either because we'd got the science or economics or issue wrong, or because we just couldn't sustain the change in real life.

So we couldn't take this final step of screening the brands of second-hand clothing for ethics, if we didn't want to run around in jute sacking like something out of *The Flintstones*.

We look forward to the day that the second-hand market is awash with sustainable brands. In the meantime, another big slice of life had altered beyond recognition. The way we think about and buy and allocate value to physical items had – just like the toiletries and food and plastic – changed fundamentally. We had got the vintage bug.

6: Loving the Preloved

Someone once described the self-made millionaire and politician Michael Heseltine as the wrong sort because he 'buys his own furniture.' In other words, he hadn't inherited vast quantities of valuable pieces from an ancestral stately pile.

The jibe said a lot about UK society then, but the fact that it usually has to be explained now says even more about 21st Century attitudes to consumption. These days new goods are seen as the right route to personal validation.

David and I are products of the yuppie 80s, mad-for-it 90s, and the global village of the 00s. Personal consumption has always been overt, ostentatious and immediate, no matter what we were buying or why.

This wasn't about fulfilling basic needs. All our adult lives our ability to buy what we want, when we want, has been the measure of our success as people. If we could nonchalantly pull out the latest phone at the bar with our mates after driving there in a shiny new motor, we were surely on a winning trajectory. The more successful, the higher the expected income and the bigger the baubles must be – if only, tragically, to avoid judgement.

I have friends who hire flashy cars to go to work meetings rather than use their own more modest family run-around. Why? Because their prospective client might draw conclusions about their ability to do their job if they don't have the trappings of a high income. They're not so concerned about having the latest gear in 'real life' they say, but worry that they won't get the deal, no matter how good they are, if they don't flaunt wealth. They're probably right.

Most people feel clothes must be new, too. In fact, so ingrained is that notion that true success is based, among other things, on the size of your wardrobe, that even characters down on their luck in film and TV always seem to wear the same clothes on repeat – at least until they make something of themselves.

To many 'thrifty' is an insult.

As a family, we have never had Hollywood budgets. But once upon a time our unit of four would spend almost exactly the national average on new clothes – around £100 a month. These days that number – even in a 'high purchase' month – is closer to £20. All of that goes on items of better, longer-lasting quality than we could have afforded brand new. It's said that 70% of the planet wears second-hand clothes. Which means 30% are missing a trick.

I was kicking myself that we haven't always shopped this way. But it turns out we kind of have. We just hadn't realised.

It took a home insurance renewal for it to dawn on us that there is only one piece of furniture in our home that we bought new. (A foot stool that the kids trashed almost immediately. I don't know why we bothered.)

I'd love to claim it was all thanks to high ideals, but the truth is that with salaries tight and student loans sitting on our shoulders for much of our early adulthood, there wasn't much cash to splash in the nearest DFS when we were setting up home – even less when the kids arrived.

But whether you compare build quality and craftsmanship or

just good old value by weight, our experience is that second-hand is usually best.

My wedding ring was my great grandmother's and my engagement ring is second-hand. Sorry, 'antique.' Both are all the more important to me for the histories they carry alongside my own. They have permanence somehow. They have borne witness to the changing fortunes of the world and its people. It is a privilege to wear them. As a bonus I haven't increased the insatiable demand for brand new bling whose extraction drives brutal devastation, pollution and exploitation across the globe.

It's not just the little things around here that have a history either. The sofa was the result of a miraculous skip dive and every chair in the house is a hand-me-down. The kitchen table was in the house when we moved in and the sitting room rug was a preloved eBay purchase identical to a dear one I'd coveted in a showroom window.

No, our home doesn't look like a catalogue shot of eerily matching interiors. It's much more personal than that.

Our kitchen and bathroom units are made from the floorboards we pulled up to fit a new heating system, the sink and taps came out of someone else's renovation, the radiators are salvage, half the furniture was left here by the previous owners and outside the hard landscaping relies heavily on a repurposed agricultural shed that couldn't cope with the weight of the previous year's snow. All in, it means our 'new' kitchen came in at £940 and refreshing the garden at £200.

So there are definite, quantifiable and fairly predictable benefits to be had from dropping out of mainstream consumption – none of which have anything to do with reclaiming a soul-destroying afternoon in an out-of-town shopping centre. (That was an added bonus.)

All our appliances are second-hand too as it turns out. And that too has far wider benefits than our bank balance.

E-Waste

With 80 million mobile phones alone in circulation among a UK population of 68 million, and more TVs than people in the average home, we're drowning in tech.

In 2019, the world threw away a record 54 million tonnes of e-waste[87] — mobile phones, stereos, televisions, fridges, microwaves, kettles, children's toys, as well as all cables, chargers, plugs and accessories. That means every man, woman and child jettisons an average of more than 7kg each every 12 months. The quantities of e-waste are increasing three times faster than the global population every year.

At almost 24kg per person per year, the UK is one of the worst culprits. We're even described by our own parliament's Environmental Audit Committee as drowning under an 'e-waste tsunami.' [88]

Nothing about the great tech throwaway makes sense to me, especially when you start looking at what makes up tech waste.

All of those apparently obsolete batteries, circuit boards and heat sinks contain an incredible amount of cobalt, aluminium and even gold and platinum.

Forget the value or even basic usefulness of the item when intact, while whole industries are intent on extracting more by destroying vast swathes of land — especially through open pit or open cast mining — we're literally throwing out £8 billion of precious metals every year.

Setting aside the fact that recycling our old tech would reward us each with hundreds of pounds worth of cold hard cash every year if we could be bothered, the throwaway 'solution' is a pretty terrible trend for the wider environment too as poisonous substances like lead and mercury seep out into the soil and water when we fail to recycle, reuse or repurpose it.

Europeans recycle about 40% of their e-waste, compared with, say, Africa where a lack of suitable infrastructure means it's usually less than 1%. But while it is better than chucking it straight into landfill, recycling last year's must-have gadget doesn't absolve us of responsibility either because the processes involved in extracting useful components release such hazardous substances directly into the environment. Often carried out thousands of miles from where the problem was created, much of it happens in the so-called 'informal' sector devoid of modern industrial processes and worker protection.

'Children are often involved in these processes, exposing them to high quantities of toxic chemicals such as lead, mercury, cadmium and dioxins, many of which can produce adverse neurodevelopmental impacts even at very low exposure levels,' warns the World Health Organisation.[89]

But it's not fair to lay this one at the feet of the consumer alone – when manufacturers constantly flood the market with new versions of models that are not designed to last. There's a name for that – planned obsolescence. Just the phrase has a sinister ring to it.

It's difficult to overstate the soaring quantities of electronics we consume and the hideous effect our tech habits have on people and places – from sourcing raw materials, through production to the pollution they cause years after we had forgotten we ever owned them.

And yet we crave more. Tech tops the nation's Christmas wish list every year regardless of whether or not any of us can tell the difference between this model and the last. As I write, an ad for the newest smartphone simply tells us to buy it so we'll 'be the envy of everyone.'

The latest, particularly damning report from the UK's Environmental Audit Committee (EAC) on e-waste even asserts that 'consumers don't have control over the products they own' after manufacturers like Apple decided to solder and glue internal components, making it almost impossible to repair them.

'Instead the charges proposed for repair by Apple in particular can be so expensive it is more economical to replace the item completely,' the cross-party committee warned.[39] The UK government has finally enshrined the right to repair into law – in a bid to 'boost a repair culture across the UK.'

Personally, we reckon the return of the repair was already on its way as consumers got sick of being bullied and coerced. In 2019 we counted a single repair cafe event in our little town – an arrangement in which participants swap hands-on expertise either in a barter or charitable donation arrangement. A year later there were four.

In our house too, the changes have been dramatic, albeit on a seemingly small physical scale. My phone, for example, is refurbished. And when, the week before the mindless consuming scrum of Black Friday, David smashed his phone by accident, we went on the hunt for a better solution.

Separating ourselves from the pursuit of shiny new tech has been far harder for David than for me. I can rarely discern much difference between the latest model of anything and its predecessor. I doubt many people can.

But as an engineer he loves the notion of clever design and ever-improving functionality. So I knew David must have struck gold after a bit of digging around online one evening when he elbowed me in the ribs and jabbed at his laptop screen. 'Look at this!' he whispered in awe. 'This is brilliant.'

'This' was a Fairphone whose design encourages you to pull it apart and fix if it goes wrong. A phone he could fix himself was the answer to David's geeky dreams. But it was also, he openly admitted, an unusual gadget he could show off to his mates – for better reasons than it being the latest version.

The immediate question was whether we could find a second-hand one. After all, the whole point is that these could and should last you for years, so did they even circulate? He went looking, and though he ultimately came up empty handed on the pre-loved front, the two month hiatus helped confirm this was the right purchase.

These days in our home second hand is the default for buying everything (well, virtually everything). We'd now only buy underwear, duvets and mattresses brand new alongside any personal hygiene products. Yes, we may be trying to do our best on the eco front, but I draw the line at a second-hand toothbrush.

One of the effects of buying this way is that it slows the whole process right down. We're as impulsive and susceptible to the endorphins of snapping up a new thing as the next family. We've been exposed to the same social norms of throwing cash at a problem, of outsourcing services, of buying ready made when we could, with some hassle and time, create a solution from our existing possessions and skills.

But there's very little in the way of immediacy in the second-hand market. By its nature, it's a process that forcibly separates the buyer from a fast fix. Making ourselves wait for the things we want or need – even if it has been by accident – has been a revelation. Transformative.

Today, our default expectation as a society is that our purchases will be delivered to our door for free the next day – an assumption that the Covid pandemic has only heightened. Retailers do everything they can, from discount countdown clocks to quasi-competition ('12 other people have this in their baskets') to part us from our cash as speedily as possible.

A key part of securing an unreturned sale is being able to put the item in our hands in the blink of an eye. Even buyer's remorse doesn't usually end up in us sending what is now 'our' possession back for a refund.

Understandably, a well-known psychological trick has now emerged in response – employed by those trying to curb their spending habits, whether that's for financial, space, environmental or other reasons. It's an easy one too. You decide you want to buy something and then wait 30 days. If you still want or need it, it's a valid purchase.

Second-hand shopping to the near exclusion of all else – when we first have to seek out the item – does that for us.

It gives us an opportunity to ask ourselves whether we actually have to purchase an item at all. Like a growing number of people, we've found ourselves stepping back from an assumption of acquisition to ask some questions first.

'Do we need it?' is only the first fork on the decision flowchart in our heads. If we do need it, can we fix or make something from items we already have? If not, can we borrow, swap or hire it?

Only if the answer is no, are we then prepared to part with cash for a second-hand item. And finally, if that option isn't available either, the purchase must be durable and, like David's new phone, fixable.

Do we miss the overwhelming choice of an entire global market touting brand new items or what we're told are unique, cutting-edge styles? Nope. Or at least not nearly enough to go back to the old ways.

I started finding myself anticipating the reuse of any new items we needed too. All else being equal, if I ever need to buy a glass jar of something for example, I'll pick up the product in the larger, more useful container.

And slowly, the knock-on effects of the great downshift made their presence felt around us in other ways.

Something weird was happening with our clothes for starters, not least that socks were coming out of the laundry in pairs – which any household knows is a miracle. And the last time we packed to go away it took roughly four minutes, including getting the small case down to the front door. But it was a while before we grasped why things were easier, faster and more organised.

Even with our determination to wring out every last use from our possessions before they are finally recycled, the slower conveyor belt of consumption meant there were more things going out than coming in.

Just like millions of other families we had masses of stuff. Stuff we didn't ever use. Stuff that had been in the same unopened box through several house moves. Stuff that only worked with other stuff we no longer had.

And gradually, over several months, our home started to give up its clutter. We realised we could see the back of the kitchen worktops and all the way under our bed. The tiny built-in wardrobe door in our bedroom now shuts.

Last time I looked I owned 50 items of clothing, including shoes, coats and accessories. And when they fail there's something quietly satisfying about finding a new use for, say, the old leather belt that now acts as a laundry peg hanger or an albeit slightly industrial looking toilet roll holder.

I've also learned to darn. And when our eldest was invited to her first fancy dress party I made her superhero outfit from material that had arrived for free from David's late grandmother. I can't tell you what a big deal that was for me because I am not a seamstress by any stretch of the imagination. It took a while, it's not quite what you'd describe as a 'professional' finish, but with her initial blazing from the thunderbolt on the cape our daughter still has it hanging on the back of her bedroom door.

I'm often asked why we've added such a lot of 'unnecessary' stress into life by going zero. But that implies mainstream consumption is easy. And yet having, buying, organising, maintaining, cleaning and eventually binning vast quantities of things is a pain in the neck that sucks up time, money, energy and, if you're in a shopping centre on a Saturday, perhaps even the will to live.

Our home is easier to organise, clean and leave than it ever has been. And when we are away from home, we're more self-sufficient with fewer belongings. We have what we need with us, belongings that we won't need to search for a bin to dispose of when we're finished with them. It's weirdly relaxing and completely unexpected.

The DIY kids' costumes and cooking from scratch do take time that we, like any other modern family, don't often feel we have but we also don't find ourselves allocating entire weekends to clearing the contents of the garage into the car to take to the recycling centre – each item tumbling into the skip along with its individual carbon footprint. Besides, we don't have a garage.

We do have a bit of space under the eaves though. It was once crammed with items I wouldn't be able to name. Now we're converting it into a secret den for the kids. Don't tell them, though: it's a surprise.

I'll level with you, the capsule wardrobe bit does leave me with fewer choices and I do sometimes think it would be nice to have a bit more variety, especially if I'm out with 'the girls' in all their finery. But that fleeting envy isn't enough of a pull.

There is a bit of an enduring eco perception problem out there, though. When most people think of zero waste or eco living, they think of bamboo sporks and stupidly expensive natural bristle brushes. Oh, and enormous 'architectural' house plants. I'm pretty sure the bandwagon-jumping price tags on all these things put real people off.

They don't trust it and I wholeheartedly agree. Those flogging the zero waste lifestyle don't seem to see the irony of suggesting that to be more environmentally responsible we must immediately go out and buy string bags, an army of kilner jars, stainless steel 'essentials' and endless supplies of the clingfilm alternative – beeswax wrap. All these brand new purchases still use materials, transport and suck up other resources regardless of their eco credentials.

We've never used a stainless steel straw, even with two tiny children in tow, and don't intend to start any time soon. And sure, we loved the idea of beeswax wrap as much as the next person, but that particular lifestyle box ticking exercise is now gathering dust in the kitchen drawer.

Don't bother. Save the resources and your money. Step away from the organic cotton bread bag. And if you decide to embark on a zero waste picnic or an al fresco working lunch, take cutlery from the kitchen drawer. Use what you have, save the resources and your money.

I am under no illusions about lucking out when I married an engineer. David has always looked at the things around him as if they're blueprints. He can see past the complete whole and not only understand how it works but also its materials and what we can use them for. I don't have that kind of brain or experience.

But I do know that this is simply a continuation of the resources mindset – the reason we tip half drunk water into the plants, or leave the oven door open after cooking to help heat the room or come up with slightly... experimental ways to use food scraps.

When the washing machine broke down we tried to fix it. When it wasn't fixable – thank you, planned obsolescence – we dismantled it, using the still alluring inner drum to make a fire pit.

There is value in everything. We just need to ignore the incessant retailer noise and work out how to use it better, smarter and more carefully. To invest in fewer, better things when we need them and view a broken or ripped or redundant item as merely at the end of its first incarnation.

We're still working towards that, especially me – the one without a practical bone in her body – but it's pretty satisfying, and in my case regularly entertaining.

And while I can see it may seem like yet another exhausting exercise in self-denial, there has been something intrinsically positive about carving out a new approach to our stuff – about learning ways to live within our means in more ways than one. Not that there's actually anything new about it – of course.

I remember my grandparents' sheds full of tools ready for a quiet fix and the remarkable knack various members of my family have of making a whole new tasty meal from leftovers and thin air. It's an art that I hope one day to master.

Meanwhile, you only take what you're going to eat in our house and you clear your plate, no matter your age, appetite, or propensity to throw a strop. And that's not just the adults. The rule applies to all of us, everywhere. We always ask to take away leftovers from restaurant or cafe meals too, however toe-curling friends and family find it. It's still a bit uncomfortable in a terribly British way, but leaving half your plate full of food or side dishes still piled high is not a sign of opulence or generosity, it's a sign of inexcusable disregard for the effort, skill and resources that made them.

If I were poetic or whimsical I might suggest that something about this feels as if we are stepping out of some manic race towards the edge of an unstable cliff and turning towards familiar firm ground. What I do know for sure is this all feels like an intrinsically good thing that makes fundamental sense. To our home, our mental health and certainly to our wallets.

There has been good news outside our little bubble too, with signs that a wider rejection of the consuming norm is under way. Just ask Marie Kondo. Or the UK's Office for National Statistics if that's more your thing, which found that although the UK population is increasing, the quantity of material consumed per person each year is dropping – from 11.3 tonnes to 7.2 tonnes in 2013.[40]

What fascinates me about those figures is that they cover the period of the financial crash, with its hit to the economy, employment and household incomes.

When the Covid pandemic hit we stopped spending and started saving astonishing amounts of cash as a nation – even with 24/7 online shopping at our fingertips and time on our hands.

When we need to, when there's an emergency, we know how to cut out excess in order to protect ourselves and our futures. Well, this is an emergency to end them all.

A life with less stuff is clearly the aspiration of the next generation coming up through the ranks. And as well as being immensely liberating, financially freeing and less stressful over all, that surely has to be a huge 'planet positive.'

In fact, the emerging trend in consumption isn't all-out purchasing – it's renting. From property to posh frocks, there is a growing body of evidence that, in response to over-consumption and the climate crisis, we're moving towards not really owning anything.

Don't take my word for it, though. Take those of the World Economic Forum and Ida Auken, the Danish MP who predicted that we would own nothing by 2030.[41] We could, she was already speculating in 2016, simply rent what we need, when we need it. We'll have kitchen equipment delivered to our door when a mixer or pasta maker is suddenly called for, and our homes would be used by others to have meetings in or work from when we're out.

It seems extreme compared with today's assumption and pursuit of ownership for its own sake. But that last bit about homes doesn't sound worlds away from the Airbnb model that has taken the world by storm. And who now buys music or movies outright rather than subscribe to a streaming service?

The sharing economy is rapidly gaining traction. Several years ago the accountants PriceWaterhouseCooper were predicting that by 2025 we would see £140bn worth of sharing industry transactions in the UK alone.[42] With the UK government pondering a tax grab of £20bn among sharing economy businesses to get us out of a massive Covid-based economic hole, even PwC's predictions are now looking conservative.

What I do know, from our own deep dive into attitudes, is that the dreams of owning the executive home, a Chelsea tractor and a crammed walk-in wardrobe are starting to feel dated.

Will our kids – income permitting – own acres of expensive, polluting, anxiety-inducing stuff? Maybe not. Maybe they won't feel the need. Maybe treading more lightly on the planet with a few more pounds in their pockets and less stuff to weigh them down will allow them to experience – rather than merely own – life in its full glory.

I hope that's true because if it is, we may have a fighting chance at all of this. But I also hope, however strongly we believe in the path David and I have chosen to take as adults, that our children are free to make those decisions for themselves.

7. Generation Fear

By the summer of 2018 our home, life and behaviours were starting to stand out. They felt different. They were different. Even our relationships with other people – with society in general – had shifted as we got into the swing of transforming our everyday choices, what we wanted from our lives and how we imagined our future.

This was the summer that we noticed that none of the adverts on TV – for washing powder, fashion labels, new furniture or fast food – related to us anymore. We stopped entering competitions because none of the prizes, such as long-haul holidays, electronic goods, a year's supply of this or that, were sustainable.

Our children had started calling out – with a certain undeniable wistfulness in their voices – the plastic toys in the ad breaks: 'Look Mummy, we don't buy those because they're plastic.' It was also the summer our eldest started school.

Apologetically, I had mentioned our stance on plastic to her teachers, clearly harassed at the start of a new year, who had already laminated everything within a mile radius by the time I got to them. And yet they were remarkably gracious, even enthusiastic.

On day one of term we had an unexpected issue, though. Our daughter had been asked to bring in a shoebox full of things that were important to her to share with the class by way of introduction. It was a nice idea. Unfortunately, it had been some time since anybody in our house had bought new shoes. Meanwhile, craft activities required cereal boxes. The fact we didn't have any cereal boxes starkly illustrated our new divergence.

We have never been particularly unusual people, always falling into a fairly predictable pattern when it came to life, family, aspiration, reward and the like. We had always ticked the same lists, shopped similar brands, pursued similar goals to everybody else.

Even after we decided to go zero, the distinctions between us and others were largely abstract while we were all at home (David and I are self-employed), muddling through with few consistent obligations outside of looking after ourselves.

It came as a shock when a new external influence showed us that our points of reference were now off compared with everyone else. For us, the start of school began a series of tiny, practical challenges that added a little extra friction to everything.

Our daughter's first term was an indicator of how much our lives had changed in a short period of time, too. When change is gradual and layered, it's difficult to realise how far you've come, especially when you're in the thick of it. While we don't believe we're swimming against the tide any more, we still often forget that our approach isn't that common until we go to friends or family's homes and are confronted by the typical supermarket shop or the plans for the next long-haul holiday. Even then we're sometimes in a bell jar of opinion about the need and will for change if not the action itself.

As we drifted into autumn, with the unsettling feeling that we were on the outside looking in for the first time, we also started to realise just how deep society's lifestyle assumptions run and how difficult they will be to alter. At their very mildest, they include an unwritten rule that we'll buy cereals from supermarkets in plastic-coated cardboard boxes containing plastic bags of food.

The eco messages we get as a society are still stuck on reducing consumption of plastic and meat. It's about not taking that new plastic bag at the supermarket or supporting token moves by big retailers. I understand why but we were some distance away from that by now. The plastic concerns in our house had by this stage zeroed in on fine details, including avoiding plastic tape on any deliveries, remembering to dodge sparkly birthday cards and managing the last of the biros.

The problem was that though the changes we had made had been huge and the effects great, we were aware that we were still fairly new to all this after just a year. Most people who live in a non-mainstream way have done so for decades, perhaps even since birth. We just weren't enough of an authority yet to confidently own the differences.

And besides, we wanted to fit in with the other parents and carers, not set our stall out as 'other.' At least not until we knew them better. I remember deliberately steering away from in-depth conversations at the school gates about what we might get the kids for birthdays and Christmas for fear of the awkward conversations it might throw up. We were well out of our depth on must-have toys and didn't want to ask – not least because we really didn't want to come across as judgemental the moment we opened our mouths.

The school is used to us these days. Last Christmas we got a phone call to discuss the use of sequins on our daughter's festive creations and teachers now bound across the playground to tell us when they've ditched the laminator and the glitter. There are even whispers of meat-free days every week for the entire place.

Of course our own integration into the school community was way down the priorities list compared with our daughter's.

Now approaching her eighth birthday, she is more than happy to state 'we don't use plastic' in a loud and confident voice. If you pushed her a little harder, she would tell you, like plenty of other kids, about plastic bags killing fish in the ocean.

In the lunch queue at school – and everywhere else for that matter – she'll hand back the plastic sachets of ketchup that keep turning up with food. When we're out, she'll turn to her little brother to tell him that we won't buy the item he is clamouring for because it is made of plastic. To his credit he usually puts it straight down, though whether that's because the sister he idolises has told him off or he's worried about turtles, it's hard to say.

But I'm not sure we should always dismiss our kids' awareness of 'the environment' so readily. It's clear that the natural world isn't a backdrop for those kids lucky enough to know it. It isn't yet another responsibility to be shouldered. Our kids beg us to let them play outside in the depths of winter – usually in the most inappropriate of summery outfits. They champion the bug hotels and the mini ponds. Bike rides are better than back-to-back *Bob the Builder* any day of the week.

Yes, our kids are young – very young. But they seem to have a clarity and an association with nature that we have lost as modern adults. It's a gap that makes it easy to imagine we live separated from nature and that protecting it is, at worst, another weighty responsibility and, at best, something nice to have. We even talk about 'getting out into nature' as if we're not biological beings ourselves. As if 'nature' doesn't run through our veins.

Our daughter has certainly made more than one adult around her stop and think. But I would be lying if I said we weren't apprehensive about how this lifestyle shift has affected the kids.

Like so many parents, we have always been clear with our children about the reasons for buying some goods but not others. Though here more than any other aspect of home life, we agonise over getting the balance right. We know we need to demonstrate the values and traits we consider important while encouraging our children to be their own people, authentic and secure in their choices, personalities and hopes. They also have to be allowed to be kids having fun without the weight of the world on their shoulders. That will come anyway.

If our daughter is given a plastic gift she's usually the first person to identify a conflict, but it's vital that she feels in charge of what she does next, including whether she keeps it or not. Sometimes she will and that has to be OK.

We're also acutely aware that because we're a little 'out of line' these days there is a risk that the kids may struggle to connect with others because of a lack of common ground, of shared social reference points.

They don't have the same toys or even accessories and I've seen the delight on our children's faces when they arrive at the homes of friends to find a world of bright, light up, all-singing, all-dancing toys. I can't blink before they're both struggling into synthetic princess gowns complete with plastic tiaras. We get it. Wooden toys and natural fibres will struggle to compete with these twinkling possibilities. No matter how full and rich your imagination, an old-school teddy can't offer a pitch perfect rendition of 'Let it go' while ice-skating – all at the touch of a button. Complete with glittering, glowing icicles.

We don't regret the lack of infuriating noise makers, though. I don't think we really appreciate how loud and bone-itchingly irritating kids' toys are until we're faced with 30 of them on a playdate – all spouting their catchphrases at once. Or worse, alone and quietly in the middle of the night as if summoning the twins from *The Shining*.

Our families and friends are itching to buy these things for the kids – the fun toys (not the horror movie characters). They want to give them that pleasure, but they generously hold back on the gifting gratification knowing we're not up for it. Of course we day-dream about raiding the local branch of a massive retailer without a care in the world, returning to give our beautiful kids all the things that their little hearts desire at that fleeting but intense moment. For a while it would be so very much fun and sometimes we do feel a bit mean in the most ridiculous, first world way.

Like every other parent, we want them to have everything. We just need to transition from what 'everything' meant for us as kids to what it needs to mean for the next generation. We all know that children don't need expensive plastic toys to play. There are numer-ous studies out there that show the fewer toys children have at their disposal, the more inventive, independent and content their play. They even seem to share better when there are fewer, not more, items to entertain them. Exploration and experience are higher on the kids' priority list than I ever realised.

Sure, that might just be our wishful thinking but there's no doubt that kids, like adults, are drowning in stuff. Though historical studies show the average child in the UK has around 230 toys at the age of 10, and plays with just 12 of them, the world's parents, grandparents, carers, friends and the rest spent almost $91 billion on children's toys alone in 2019 – and that's before we get started on all the clothes, tech, equipment and other items.[43]

And yet it keeps coming – not just on birthdays and Christmas but on high days, holidays and every other day it seems. Going to see a family movie, children's play or the panto? You'll be a terrible parent if you don't buy the plastic prop to augment your viewing pleasure.

When we took the children to see the carnival passing through town last winter, the flanking carts of expensive but flimsy light-up toys, formed in such a way that you can't even change the batteries to extend their lives a little, seemed more of a focal point to the chilly crowd than the wagons of carefully created spectacle they'd come to see.

You can't even buy a meal or snack – a quick burger or little chocolate egg without a cheap plastic gimmick arriving as standard. Quantity and novelty, we are taught from a very young age, are goals in themselves, regardless of whether the item is wanted.

No wonder there are kids out there begging for the end of the crap plastic giveaway. In 2019, Ella and Caitlin McEwan and Jacob Douglas (aged nine, seven and eight respectively) coaxed McDonalds into reducing, but sadly not removing, plastic toys from its Happy Meals, which the children repeatedly pointed out are only ever played with for a few minutes. More than a billion are handed out every year.

Only in late 2021, after years of pressure, did the brand state that each Happy Meal toy sold anywhere in the world would be made of renewable and recycled materials. But only by 2025.

In our house, it has undoubtedly been far harder to exclude plastic from our children's lives and bedrooms than anywhere else, which is particularly disturbing given the impact these things will have on their world and their lives long after the designers, manufacturers, marketers and purchasers of those items are dead and buried.

At the same time the intimidating army of other new parents, now close friends, have started asking us for alternative product recommendations and tips on reducing waste. They tell us of their determination to ensure their next round of birthday party bags is entirely plastic free. It's brilliant, especially as party bags are such a clear example of how we are held back by that invisible assumption barrier.

Nobody wants to be the first to stop handing the damned things out, mostly over worries about the judgement. And let's face it, parents judge. One friend recently asked party guests not to bring a physical birthday gift for his already over-catered-for seven-year-old. If they really weren't comfortable about turning up empty handed, he said they could contribute towards a bike upgrade that the child actually wanted. He was brutally shot down. When the tiny but vocal guests then left without the usual quantities of bright plastic only really designed for the bin, the whole thing became the stuff of infamy. I don't think the experiment was ever repeated.

We had finally put our heads above this particular parapet by the time of our daughter's fifth birthday – that one in the woods with the controversial marshmallows. We'd avoided the balloons and the shiny decorations. There wasn't a jaunty throwaway plastic tablecloth, themed pack of napkins or even plastic-wrapped, palm-oil filled sweet, chocolate or games prize to be seen. We were in the woods, not the village hall. In other words, we'd slyly taken the cowards' way out of the problem by changing the setting.

But we couldn't quite get past the party bag compulsion. Instead, each child received a reusable cotton bag containing a second-hand book about games to play in the woods. The disappointment was palpable. The adults had a great afternoon – ignoring the increasingly feral children and prodding the fire with a beer and an ill-placed sense of combustion competence. But some of the kids may never forgive us for the lack of take home treasure.

When the last birthday was a Zoom party thanks to lockdown it was a relief, even if we did feel the compulsion to promise that we'd 'make up for it after Covid' like every other primary school parent.

But we're not just worried about the kids being in on the latest craze or demonstrating largesse to pint-sized guests. Our children have coloured pencils instead of felt tip pens. That's partly, I'll be honest, because the sofa would never be the same again but mostly it's because felt tips are plastic – a kind of invisible plastic we never really saw before. Have I irrationally worried that their creativity may be hindered because there isn't a plastic pot of PVA or a glue stick around? Sure I have. Have the children noticed? Unlikely.

Like every other parent, we are working hard to support our children in being happy, confident, thoughtful people well-armed with the skills and emotional balance to make it as independent individuals.

We may find that by the time they're in their teens they reject our family approach. As young adults, they may need a more straightforward way of living. As parents themselves, the world may look so fundamentally different anyway that the details of our lives today are redundant and archaic. We know we will have to accept those decisions like all the parents that have gone before us who have watched their children disappear off into the wide world.

But we cannot get away from the realities they face in that world – and this one.

According to the UN, one in every four childhood deaths is related to pollution. As I write, a landmark ruling in the UK has directly linked air pollution to the death of a young girl. It is now a matter of fact, not emotive liberal hyperbole, that the way we live is killing our children. Not somewhere else or at some time in the distant future when we're long gone. This week. In London.

Since becoming parents we have come to believe that protecting the environment is part of the same wider obligation to care for our children as holding their hands to cross the road. We do both to try to ensure they remain safe and healthy, instilling behaviours that will protect them from danger and difficulty especially when we are no longer there to pull them out of harm's way.

I've never had the guts to say that out loud to the other parents we know, but something has changed. The accelerating speed at which our collective lifestyle is affecting our children here and now means we have to be bold. There is no time left to be polite about this.

I was once asked during a radio interview if our kids are worried about not having the latest plastic toy or, when they're older, the latest phone. Personally, I suspect the concerns we voice over whether our kids could deal with changing their habits is much more of a reflection on us than them.

When I last asked our daughter about how she feels about protecting the environment she said that people didn't care but didn't know why. Maybe, she speculated, it's too hard.

Children and young adults are clearly frustrated and anxious. Four in every five children in the UK are worried about the impact that climate change will have on them when they're older. Their fears are so great that a study for the BBC found a fifth of 8-16 year olds have even had nightmares on the subject.[44]

Most of them simply don't trust adults to accept and tackle the complex but critical challenges that climate change, pollution and species depletion present. Two thirds say leaders aren't listening to their views.

Time and time again, the world's youngest demographics have demonstrated that they have the loudest, clearest voices on our climate emergency. They understand what it means and they want no part in it. They aren't burdened with infuriating, diluting, excuse-ridden grey areas the rest of us feel obliged to inhabit.

You can see why the school strikers are compelled to shout about their education being pointless if there isn't a secure world. They are afraid, but it must feel like they're shouting their deep, fundamental, entirely rational fears into a dense pillow of what, logistics? Short-term gain from investment in industries with no future? Laziness? That must be the scariest thing of all. Truthfully, it is for us and we're only expected to survive a few more decades.

Neither David or I, nor any other parent can alter the historic damage that has been done to the world. No matter how fast or infuriatingly slowly we turn this ship around, our children will grow

Eco-anxious

'Talking to children about climate change gives a fresh perspective on the absurdity of doing so little about the climate emergency and also highlights for young people the troubling disconnect between what politicians say and what they do,' argued Caroline Hickman, of the University of Bath's Department of Social and Policy Sciences when her latest study found eco-anxiety was affecting more children than ever before.[90]

'On the one hand, the UK Parliament votes for a climate emergency, whilst on the other it votes to expand an airport. In Brazil, scientists conclude that the Amazon is the world's best store for climate-warming CO_2, yet large swathes of it are burned deliberately to make room for the feed for methane-belching cattle and other livestock, if not for the animals themselves.

'And in Australia, despite warnings, a vast coal mine gets approved near the Great Barrier Reef. Broken promises and inaction coupled with the enormity of the climate crisis are all beginning to take their toll on children's mental health,' she warned. And that is more of a concern for us as parents than temporary playground ostracism.

up and grow old in a depleted environment. We and others are eternally sorry for that.

What we can do now though, is help them form the connections between our individual choices and the decisions made by central governments about runways and deforestation and coal mines.

We talk about the environment with the kids, from the pot on the windowsill or the mangrove swamps in a country they've never seen, though we spare them the grisly details, the deadly predictions over their futures. When we make changes or they spot differences between us and their friends' families, we include them, we give them that all-important voice and explain, in age-appropriate language, why we are taking action.

Demonstrating that we as adults are prepared to do all we can to pursue different choices – to keep pushing – may be all we can do. But it also strikes us that if we can help our children take ownership of their actions we may be able to help them re-package their anxieties. We may be able to distil those concerns and fears into a positive force for good. Maybe, just maybe, we can empower them. Or, more accurately, support them in empowering themselves.

Our kids may not be able to read the academic papers on ocean acidity or socio-economic theses but our hope is that they know something more important than that. If we have achieved anything so far, I hope we have demonstrated to our children that we are not sitting by while urging others to take action. I hope they know that we are serious about doing our bit and won't shy from our responsibilities when things get uncomfortable.

As they get older and begin to grasp the nuance of what is happening around them, we will help them to address fears about the threats and dangers we all face. But I don't believe, if they do choose to continue to live as we do now, that they will be outsiders for long. They already aren't.

Evidence of change is everywhere you care to look. Plant-based dishes appear on almost every menu, even in the most unlikely venues. Carrying a single use plastic bottle is becoming socially unacceptable, replaced with refillables.

These are tiny gestures. But they are surely the beginnings of true, fundamental change.

Now more than ever, we are convinced that while our children's futures will be challenging in ways we cannot imagine, there is a collective will to live differently. To do better. There needs to be, because right now so many of the milestones and celebrations in our lives are marked by the complete opposite – a reality-dodging level of consumption so accepted, so assumed, so expected, that we barely register it as fundamentally destructive to our financial and even mental health, as well as to our environment.

8. Throw Away Tradition

Our son was sure it was going to snow in time for Christmas Day. We tried to suggest it might not happen and that it was still a special day even without a blanket of white, but he wasn't having it.

Needless to say, it wasn't a white Christmas. In fact, the UK Met Office now forecasts that within just 20 years global heating will mean most of southern England won't dip below freezing. No more snowmen or tobogganing or the unexpected, unadulterated joy of a snowy day off school. And those are the tiny manifestations of the climate crisis compared with the monumental impact on our flora and fauna. If you stop and think about that too hard it is devastating, not least in its proximity.

Our son's automatic associations between traditional annual celebrations and the spectacles of the natural world isn't lost on us. Nor is the irony.

At Easter, the shops are crammed full of our traditional fare – lamb. That makes sense initially – Easter is all about new life and rebirth. But that's when lambs are born, not slaughtered. Lamb eaten at Easter (unless shipped from New Zealand) has to be born in the depths of winter to feed our now seriously disjoined seasonal associations.

An alien landing in the UK during winter festivals, particularly a 21st Century Christmas, would be even more confused. So, I suspect, would the Victorians. Why are we marking the turning of the seasons, the return of light or the birth of a king by decorating our homes with plastic imitations of real plants that are probably nearby?

Whether you're decking your halls with prickly reminders of Christ's crown of thorns, harking back to the burning of holly and ivy during the pagan festival of Beltane or, like us, just decorating the house for Christmas, it makes sense to do it with evergreen, abundant, fast-growing and, in the case of ivy and mistletoe, parasitic species that have featured in our landscape for hundreds if not thousands of years. For free.

Our street and small back garden teem with holly and ivy. With those holly berries offering much needed food for birds, and the ivy providing vital shelter when all else has died off, we try not to get carried away.

Getting back to reality definitely helped us navigate our first attempt at a zero waste Christmas back in 2017 and four years later, we're still learning. Last year we had a go at making a wreath out of the inside ring from a decrepit lampshade. It wasn't the most beautiful door decoration on the street. If truth be told it looked like an old bird's nest but that, I was duly informed by the kids, wasn't the point.

If you ask me, though, the big bonus of real greenery is that we don't need to store it in our limited space for the other 50 weeks of the year, it's straight on the compost or, later, on the fire to warm the house as we clean and clear the house in the grey of early January – something that appeals to the medieval peasant in me. It hasn't happened yet, but if anyone were to show up on our doorstep with a proper yule log they'd have a friend for life.

What does hang about are the three potted fir trees. Bought just once, for the same price as a felled one, living bought and rented trees have become stormingly popular.

Granted, something about them sitting on the patio in the middle of July jars a bit. They struggle to thrive under our black thumbs but it helps that we live at the right latitude and longitude to dabble in an old school approach to Christmas, especially as these trees have travelled less than three miles to their current spot. I keep expecting Mr Tumnus to trot by our miniature woodland.

We know that tinsel, glitter-covered baubles and table confetti bestow a sparkly wonder on Christmas. But if we plumped for them the contents of the vacuum cleaner would have to go in a bin rather than the compost – and we don't miss them enough for that.

Our decorations are either the same glass or felt ones we've had for years or, if we fancy an update, paper. Remember those interlocking chains we all made as kids? There are a lot of those in our house. One year we got a bit ambitious with the YouTube paper star tutorials, but I notice that faffy activity hasn't become a family tradition.

You can now buy paper chain kits but like many households we just raid the recycled paper stack. If we send cards, which we try not to do in favour of a call, they are cut outs from the kind messages we received last year. The kids love it. One of my favourite Christmas memories is an unexpected day off when my daughter pulled the classic vomited-once-and-totally-fine-but-can't-go-back-to-school-for-two-days thing so we gave up and spent the day making Christmas cards from last year's offerings.

Decorating the house is the easy bit.

We follow the same rules for food at Christmas time as we do the rest of the year. Everything is made from scratch, and because we tend to mainline mince pies if we're not careful, we've been known to start baking in November just to see us through. One member of the family magically supplies a homemade Christmas pud each year. It's a proper festive miracle – the same person never seems to do it twice, it is never discussed or timetabled and yet we never go without and never double up. That's my kind of miraculous.

Thankfully, cooking seasonable and local food is far easier at Christmas than most other times of year. (Easter, falling right in the hunger gap, is more challenging.)

Meanwhile, like every other celebrating family, we'll include a treat or two. So while there is some cheese at Christmas it was made 30 miles away, we pick it up in our own containers, the amount we buy now lasts a month rather than two days and instead of grapes flown in from South Africa it's accompanied by a jar of chutney.

Any extras, after we get through the weird combo curries, go in the freezer, especially any bones because who can be bothered to make stock on Boxing Day? We do love a bit of leftovers conjuring though. Making something out of what seems like nothing, for free, especially after a season of spending, definitely appeals.

Above all we try not to over-cater. Our first lockdown Christmas prompted us to carve up a turkey and share it out between isolating households, so only a leg came home. It was perfect for one adult and two children. We just didn't need any more.

Our Christmas food spend as a zero waste household is half what it was when we were 'normal.' Last year, with peelings and trimmings feeding a relative's chickens, the only things that went in the compost bin were coffee granules and tea leaves.

Then there's the matter of gifts. That took a bit more psychological unpacking.

On Christmas Eve 2018 I stood in our children's bedroom, holding my breath in case they woke up, with two hessian sacks in my hands. Boldly printed with an attempt at a North Pole stamp, they were purchases made years before in a flurry of 'special spending' that would surely make our children's Christmas experience more majestic.

That night they were half as full as they had been the year before and I felt terrible. I couldn't get past the memory of peeping towards the end of my own bed as a small girl to see gifts overflowing from my own and having that effervescent sense of absolute, all-encompassing magic.

Never mind that my 'sack' had actually been a pillowcase less than half the size of these modern novelties, as an adult I was standing there in the dark listening to my children's snuffles worried that fewer items translated into less childhood magic. It wasn't true and maybe, as all those studies around the number of children's toys imply, the opposite is, in fact, correct. But I struggled to shake it off and – though scaling back helps us on the road to going zero at Christmas – I still do.

We made a conscious decision to dramatically cut down on the number of gifts, and treats and extras we bought for Christmas. We definitely wouldn't, we decided, simply buy things for the sake of making up the numbers or adhering to yet more of those unspoken, perhaps even imaginary social rules.

After years of David and I trying to outdo each other, or at least go one better than the previous year in the 'main present' stakes, we decided to scale down the gift to each other. We ditched everything but a small stocking, which definitely helps take the pressure off. And that has to be made up of modest items.

At Christmas and any other gift-giving time, we try to plump for an experience rather than a physical thing, partly in a bid to reduce our use of all that wrapping paper and tape – even if it is paper-based.

Last year, undeterred by the experience of that brave friend whose clever birthday party gift appeal was smashed to pieces, we

A time for taking

Named the world's worst
annual environmental
disaster, we create 30
per cent more waste at
Christmas on top of our
usual throwaways.
We use 227,000 miles of
wrapping paper each year
attached with 50 million rolls

Freestocksorg, Pexels

of tape, send 33 million trees' worth of cards, throw away
seven million tonnes of perfectly edible food complete with
125,000 tonnes of plastic food wrap. That includes two
million turkeys and £48m worth of unwanted gifts.

Those gifts aren't the ones that make it to the charity
shop or are sold, returned, re-gifted or recycled, they're just
the ones that go straight in the bin. All but 1% of Christmas
crackers are in the bin by the end of Christmas day. With
more than ten million people in the UK going into debt to
cover Christmas, spending £10 or more on crackers is, in our
view, rubbish.

And then there's the prickly matter of the tree.

The Carbon Trust reckons a two-metre tree without a
root ball that goes into landfill in January will produce a
carbon footprint of around 16kg CO2e, akin to three return
flights from London to Australia, as well as the particularly
damaging greenhouse gas methane. But if it has roots and
you plant it, burn it or have it chipped, that drops to around
3.5kg – most of which comes from transporting shrubbery
around the country.

A fake tree made from plastic has a massive carbon
footprint of 40kg, though, which means you would have

to use it for at least ten years to level up on a responsibly-disposed-of real one on the carbon stakes alone. Then there's the impact of the plastic itself. Unfortunately, each year 14% of all the UK's synthetic trees are dumped along with seven to eight million real ones, which break down in the anaerobic conditions of the typical landfill.

A growing number of UK consumers — especially those based in cities — are quite taken with the idea of a rented living tree, especially because it gets delivered to your door and picked up after the big day to be cared for and re-rented 12 months later.

clubbed together with the grandparents, aunts and uncles to buy our son a replacement bike rather than each couple handing over something individually. We wrapped it in sheets and tied it with ribbon that were returned to the cupboard and kids' craft box respectively afterwards.

Other physical gifts too are often wrapped in material that forms part of the gift. Though it used to cause some confusion over whether we expected the material back or not, we now get reports of what the particularly creative members of the clan have done with them. It's impressive. Anything that is still paper-wrapped is held together with a reusable ribbon (also fished out of the craft box) rather than single-use tape.

If we do go for physical gifts, it goes without saying that within our own household everyone receives second-hand or refurbished items as default at Christmas and any other time. And because they don't have the brand new price tag, we can pick up higher quality, longer-lasting items for the same budget. This preloved approach has definitely taken some bravery to implement for aunts, uncles, parents and friends.

For a while we skirted the issue by either not telling them their gifts had a history or presenting them with upcycled items. One Christmas, several people received washbags made of reused material. Not made by me or David, rather by someone more talented who lives on our street.

These days we have a few more zero waste Christmases, birthdays, weddings and the rest under our belts. Our families and friends have got used to what we're trying to do, how and why. We're happy to acknowledge our vintage buys. Last Christmas our newest nephew received a child's wooden chair, made in the 1930s, instead of something brand new. Fingers crossed his parents agreed that its heritage made it more rather than less special. Luckily, they're too polite to tell us if they didn't.

At Christmas, invisible plastic still regularly trumps us, though. It usually comes in the form of advent calendars with cellophane covers, plastic coated cardboard outer sleeves and plastic vacuum formed trays. Even with several wooden and material refillable versions at home they still keep turning up thanks to well-meaning relatives. Last year the dog even got one, complete with 24 individually plastic-wrapped treats.

A lot of the effort in keeping plastic out of our lives now depends on successfully heading off friends and family from purchases like these. In this case we were just too late and once bought, it was all we could do to ask again that the children don't receive throwaway versions next year.

There are no pre-prepared snacks, selection boxes or tins of chocolates with their individual plastic wrappers in our house at Christmas. Which has the added bonus of saving us from ourselves. If we do ever receive these things as gifts we either carefully refuse them if we feel we can without causing offence, hand them on to people we know would go out and buy them anyway or take them to food bank collections.

Christmas, above all other dates in the diary, highlights how fine a line we're walking between offending people we love and doing what we think is right. We wobble off it more than we'd like.

We realise that we must be a total nightmare to buy presents for and while trying to demonstrate our gratitude, we do try to suggest that it's really not necessary to get us anything. Not in an attention-seeking-great-auntie-who-doesn't-actually-mean-it way, but because actually we don't need any more stuff. Or, we suggest somewhat artlessly, we could do something together in lieu of a physical gift. If it involves good food and easy drinkers, we're all onto a winner.

That all leaves us with one recurring problem that we struggle with all year round but above all during special occasions. The invisible plastic – the items that are so ingrained in our lives we don't even register them anymore. It scuppers us time and time again.

One Christmas our son received a lovely carefully considered wooden plane, twice. One giver had removed the plastic wrapper before handing it over, the other hadn't but we can understand the thinking behind both approaches.

The invisible plastic is frustrating, but more importantly it is incredibly difficult to know how best to sail such emotive waters. We have such generous and kind people around us who simply want us to have lovely things, especially the children. Who would want or consider themselves so superior as to throw those sentiments back at them as somehow unwanted or, worse, not good enough, because they don't make it through a labyrinthine set of eco criteria? We sometimes find Christmas shopping a time-consuming, compromise-laden headache.

But against the backdrop of a global crisis, and not least because hitting the shops was suddenly risky, 2020 was the year the automatic habits really started to feel ridiculous. Not to mention, as unemployment figures rose, unnecessarily expensive. Across the country, the Covid Christmas spend was down more than £10bn on the year before.

As a family, our Christmas spending is down more than £1,000 a year from its peak. In fact, our whole extended family has cut back noticeably over recent Christmases, with much relief come the credit card statement in January. Above all, we all know that if we do receive a gift it has been carefully chosen, it's not just making up the numbers.

It's not just the family either. Fed up of struggling to furnish every cousin in her enormous family with the best ever gift, one friend is on a mission to start a secret Santa among the adults for the ever-expanding army of children instead of each presenting yet more things that the overwhelmed offspring will either struggle to concentrate on or quickly dismiss.

Several of the other parents in our group of friends that fell into the trap of getting each other's children something each year have suggested a summer picnic instead.

At the height of the pandemic, Oxfam research suggested half the country was considering buying second-hand gifts, saving an average of £200 each in the process. Seventy per cent of Brits are now shopping more sustainably than five years ago. Maybe we have been worrying unnecessarily about what people will think of our preloved gifting after all.

Our family and friends know what we're trying to do and are incredibly supportive. Even so, at Christmas, on birthdays, anniversaries and other significant dates, we end up receiving items we wouldn't buy ourselves because of their materials, origins, impact or all three. We also end up with sellotape, shiny plastic-coated wrapping paper, and sometimes that hoover-loving glitter on cards or sequins on clothes.

Halloween and bonfire night is undoubtedly the toughest period to navigate in our house, though. Festivals bring with them endless wrapped sweets, synthetic dressing-up clothes, ghoulish plastic props and cellophane-wrapped bangers, sparklers and Catherine wheels.

I have a picture of our daughter as a rosy-cheeked two-year-old sitting on our front step surrounded by fake flickering plastic candles (safety first) dressed head to toe in a pink polyester witch's outfit, sparkly pink hat falling over her eyes, handing out individually packaged sweets from a hard plastic pumpkin-shaped bucket to other children (also encased in flammable materials.)

Yet again our cultural traditions whose key identifying features are heavily reliant on seasonal, native, natural life – in this case the abundance of pumpkins in October – had been hijacked by the margin-seeking middle men determined to replace the natural freebies with artificial buys. Needless to say, the toddler in the picture was having a ball. We all were. We played out the same rituals every year, never really thinking too much about what was right in front of us.

These days All Hallows' Eve is heavily reliant on loose, unadorned pick 'n' mix, homemade costumes, a firepit (grown ups only) and actual pumpkins we then live off for a week. Without realising it, we were starting to draw upon some of the traditions of the old festival of Samhain whose supposedly cleansing fires and offerings of food and drink once marked the end of the harvest and the start of the dark half of the year. Spooky.

We wouldn't ask our friends or family to share our approach and we certainly wouldn't ever try to force them. Besides, the people around us make enormous efforts to fit in with our choices. Recent years have seen birthday presents sent in re-usable material bags and even homemade hand-stamped designs on reused brown paper tied up with string.

Though the last few years have led to only a handful of plastic tape being binned, a truly zero waste festival seems almost impossible. At least for the moment.

Quite a few people we know well and who know us well assume that we 'don't quite mean everything' when we say we try not to use plastic, let alone the additional environmental steps we've taken since. They tend to be dismissive, especially older relatives, and arrive brandishing gifts, with flowers in a cellophane sleeve or chocolates that they thought were 'fine because it's just the wrapper.' Their gifts are generous and well-meant, but we're left with more plastic.

One close member of our family, standing in our kitchen only last week, went looking for the bin to get rid of the wrapper from a box of biscuits she had kindly brought round. 'I hadn't realised you really don't have a bin at all,' she muttered, bewildered as she pivoted on the spot to double check the corners of the room. In the end, she stuffed the wrapper in her pocket.

Others took a slightly more aggressive approach once they realised we were serious about doing things a bit differently – typically calling us out for our other eco failings or historical attitudes. While we're used to that response now, one of the biggest ongoing challenges is trying to make it clear that the choices we make are not a reflection on anyone else.

We're trying to do what we think is right, going as far as we believe we can in our own lives. But that's it. Like every other human on the planet, we're just trying to get on with it, we don't exist to highlight 'failings' in other peoples' lives. That kind of evangelism wouldn't get us anywhere fast. Anyway, we know we don't get it right. We know we have much more to do. The truth is that most of our headspace is taken up trying to continue the unravelling, learning process for ourselves, let alone anyone else. This is a surprisingly personal journey.

Plus, we are managing a real family, not an Instagram account. Nobody needs another twit flogging some unattainable image of 360-degree perfection. It puts people off making changes themselves.

By accident, our little household seems to have ended up with simpler, cheaper festivities and events that are less stressful, less destructive and afford us more downtime during them. Hopefully without upsetting anybody. But the fact that it's not just us is massive.

Sure we're still out on a bit of a limb at the moment socially, but that limb is growing and strengthening. It's being joined by other branches all the time.

If only because a lot of this is now normal behaviour for us, and we know there is a growing number of other people making some of the same changes, the gap feels like it is closing, not widening – especially, somewhat ironically at consumption-heavy Christmas.

That means we feel like we can do more, we can go further. Only that regularly means not going anywhere at all.

9: Seeing It All

It's early 2019 and I'm sitting in yet another nondescript services on the M5 so frustrated and tired that I'm going to throw something. Ideally, the husband who got us into this mess. Ideally, out of the window into a greasy puddle. The cold rain is dripping down the windows but you can't see it billowing across the car park because it is pitch black.

The kids have finally fallen asleep through sheer exhaustion, sitting upright in the most uncomfortable looking positions known to man after what felt like hours of fatigue-induced whingeing. We have been in the car for four and a half hours and we were still just that little bit too far from home to make it in one charge.

We are travelling home from a weekend in the bright lights of London town, about 150 miles away. Normal people living normal lives would have done it in three hours. They would have been tucked up in bed hours ago. We on the other hand had one more stop to do first so it was going to take us six hours to cover the same ground. David was the one who had convinced me this was the right car for us, so I was now contemplating divorce on those grounds.

In the UK, legislation that makes the sale of a new combustion engine vehicle illegal after 2030 is the final nail in the coffin for a diesel and petrol world that was already starting to fall out of favour.

But what kind of idiots decide a fully electric car is a good idea at the end of 2018? What particular brand of moron with young children and typically fraught lives then realise they can't afford a top of the range Tesla and, instead of swapping their dirty diesel for a conscience-soothing if rather ineffectual hybrid like sane motorists, stick to their arbitrary set of life rules and instead pitch for a 2016 Nissan Leaf with battery life to match. 100 mile range my arse.

The electric motor isn't the problem. It was so efficient to start with that the technology has barely changed since the 19th Century. The limitation has always been storing enough juice in the battery to be able to do anything sensible. And ours was being left behind.

The first, very important, point to make is of course that battery technology has come on so fast and so far since then that an unwanted and yet intimate knowledge of the nation's Welcome Breaks probably won't be a reality for the 12 million UK motorists who state that their next car purchase will be fully electric.

To them, range anxiety may not be a soul-gnawing distraction where every gentle incline, especially if it is cold and raining, has you nervously checking the distance to the next recharge. But in February 2019 it was for us. It was the reason we had crawled along at 63 mph exactly for the whole wretched journey, looking for the next big lorry whose slipstream we could ride like the turtles in *Finding Nemo*. Despite these efforts we would still have to stop four times. Chilled out we were not. This was a normal long distance journey too.

Luckily the popularity of the EV was still on the cool side back then and there wasn't another soul at any of the charging points we now plot our travelling lives around to slow us down even further.

If there had been that particular day I would have tumbled the children into the nearest Travelodge and worried about finishing the journey another time. By train.

These days, though it adds hours to already long journeys, there's something very heartening about pulling up to a bank of chargers. Instead of being stared at as we plug in, we're instantly part of an ever-growing throng split almost equally between those motorists with an eye on climate change and those with an eye on their wallets. Almost before you've stepped onto the tarmac there's a comment or two hurled your way, usually about how to use the charging point. If you really strike up a chat, you swap tips on the best apps for calculation range. Except for drivers of Jaguar's EV, the iPace, who never seem to want to join in. Perhaps they're more used to the VIP treatment, but I will never get tired of the default priority parking. Most charging points are as close to buildings as possible to keep infrastructure costs down. One day, possibly very soon, that will change as the world goes electric and they become more than a novelty, but for now I'll happily cruise past the little old ladies in National Trust car parks.

I can't argue with our savings either – around 80% of the running costs for our old diesel in light of both government incentives and, more importantly, no petrol station visits.

Don't tell David, but on a few summers' evenings, there is even something absurdly relaxing about taking forever to get to our destination. We have no choice but to stop regularly on long journeys and stretch our legs while the battery charges. The kids certainly benefit from us being unable to do 400 miles in one frantic push. A snail's pace on the motorway also means we get the chance to have the odd proper conversation that isn't a snatched strategy for the next set of life logistics.

While plotting routes and making plans based on charging points along the A303 doesn't immediately sound like an adventure, it sometimes means taking roads less travelled and discovering new pub beer gardens.

There's also something quite calming about pulling off without the rev of an engine and idling in silence.

Of all the changes we have made, the switch to an EV is one of those taken up by the friends and family around us with most enthusiasm. With their up-to-date battery technology, more recent converts are unlikely to have a creeping sense of range anxiety before they have left the services slip road. With the newest vehicles really starting to close the range gap between electric and combustion engines, and coming in at comparable prices, there are only positives – on carbon emissions, running cost, tax incentives and driving experience. Or at least so it seemed to me. But to be sure this was the right call, I really needed to understand what was going on under the bonnet.

Today's drivers trying to do the right thing continue to face a complex and opaque decision. For us, the fall into a decision-making rabbit hole was only marginally alleviated – and not without confusion – by purchasing a second-hand EV and always recharging from renewably sourced electricity.

Meanwhile, we signed up to test a vehicle to grid trial – an experiment that assesses the viability of using electric vehicles effectively as a network of storage batteries that feeds into the National Grid during high demand. David revels in the geekiness of it all. It's the first thing that comes up in conversation with people he hasn't seen in a while, rather than how the kids are doing in school. At least we got a free charger out of it all.

Non-combustion engines may be the only choices from 2030 but none of the new housing going up around us has EV chargers, which surely makes them unfit for purpose right about now. A call to our local council suggests the construction firms concreting over nearby fields have no obligation to include them and, at a cost of £900 each, none has bothered unless strong-armed into it. Which wasn't happening. At least such obligations have been made law recently.

We, however, now have a big white box on the side of our house – the equipment required for the trial – alongside a much more manageable everyday charger. Nothing on our journey to zero is unaffected it seems – not even how our house looks from the street. It is certainly the first thing delivery drivers ask about.

I'm just pleased we've graduated from the slightly Heath Robinson extension lead across the pavement set-up that we didn't dare plug in until the middle of the night in case the cord sent some unsuspecting pedestrian flying and we were sued.

That in itself was an improvement on the nightly, soul-destroying trip to the nearest motorway services to recharge when we couldn't get a parking space outside our house. At no point did we anticipate that being greener would mean spending so much time at motorway services. We follow the plans for lamppost recharging points and other network infrastructure with interest, occasionally wondering if anyone has thought about trip hazards.

Then there's the campervan. We love it. We love everything about it. We lived in it for three months one endless summer and it hasn't been the same since. We don't care if it is in less than pristine condition or that it's a more modest T25 cousin to the immaculate bay windows and splitties that grace the summer shows. But we do care about its carbon emissions.

With no sign yet of the second-hand EV van of our dreams, we've gone in feet first to convert ours – doing it all ourselves to avoid a crippling £60,000 bill, and replacing it with merely a massive one. It turns out there's a reason few people embark on this kind of project unless it's their paid employment.

Even doing it all ourselves and sourcing every component second-hand, the batteries required to convert this hulk of a vehicle

A greener highway

It appears insanely difficult to work out just how virtuous, or not, an EV is compared with a conventional combustion engine vehicle.

The lifetime emissions of our Leaf, for example, are regularly quoted at around three times lower than those of a conventional car per mile – before taking into account how the electricity to run it is generated throughout its life. But that kind of comparison is based on calculations including driving patterns and even the weather. Unless you happen to be carbon counting king Mike Berners-Lee, you'd be mad to attempt a universal estimate between traditional, hybrid or fully electric vehicles.

The production of any car results in carbon emissions – whether it's shipping components around the world or smelting bodywork steel. Having such a resource-rich battery means more carbon emissions are emitted during the production of an electric car than for a diesel or petrol vehicle. And not by a few per cent either – by more than a third, according to some studies.

The emissions around battery production seem to vary dramatically too – again depending on the study. But it's a pretty important factor as battery cost falls and our vehicles contain larger batteries with longer range.

Plus, just like their small appliance peers, rechargeable car batteries catalyse the same environmental and human catastrophes when it comes to mining lithium, cobalt and other metals and minerals.

Half a million tonnes of lithium has been extracted in the last 10 years[91] as the global demand for EVs has soared. But the market's growth to date is nothing. The United Nations Conference on Trade and Development (UNCTAD) estimates that the global rechargeable car battery market — worth a little over $7 billion (£5.2 billion) in the middle of 2020 — will explode to more than £58 billion by 2024.

Rathaphon Nanthapreecha, Pexels

While the lithium involved catches the most headlines, nickel and cobalt are pretty intimidating battery bedfellows too. UNICEF has warned as much as a fifth of the cobalt produced in the Democratic Republic of Congo (DRC) — which accounts for around two thirds of the world supply — is sourced from artisanal mines where up to 40,000 children work for low pay in hazardous conditions.[92]

The industry is looking for ways to reduce its dependence on such raw materials, develop more sustainable mining techniques and recycle spent lithium-ion batteries. With the potential returns so high, there are several secretive research and development projects under way across competing materials technology firms.

Right now, for example, with lithium's volatility and tendency to amalgamate making lithium extraction from batteries a long and complex process, it remains cheaper to pull it out of the ground than to recycle. It's also faster than pursuing potential alternative battery technologies, such as solid state carbon options that charge instantly, degrade slowly and have no lithium or cobalt component.

Better solutions may be coming down the motorway, but they're still a long way off.

suck up between £10,000 and £15,000 and the motor another £4,000 to £10,000. David is loving the intricacy of this mammoth job. The truth is we've already been working on this for a year and yet we always seem to be at least six months away from being able to cruise down to the nearest beach on little more than a prevailing wind.

All of which begs the question 'What about hydrogen fuel cells?' Just the phrase will always remind me of the scene in *Back to the Future* where Doc refuels the DeLorean with banana skins and beer.

There's something very simple about the idea of producing energy by smashing hydrogen and oxygen together. One big selling point of fuel cell EVs (or FCEVs if you're after pub chat points), is that they don't need a massive bank of those expensive, environmentally disastrous batteries because they produce their own electricity rather than storing it from an external source.

Inside the fuel cell, hydrogen reacts with oxygen in a process known as reverse electrolysis to produce electrical energy and heat along with water, which, in a car, slips out of the exhaust as vapour. That makes them emissions free – at least at the point of use – as the energy either powers the vehicle or is stored for later use in small battery.

A tank of hydrogen can be topped up in a few minutes, just like filling up a combustion engine car, and typically offers a longer range than that of a standard electric vehicle.

Hydrogen cars have been around for years, but are still few in number. Unfortunately, we don't have the £60,000 or more required to own one of the two models currently available. The size of the tank required and small-scale production, among other factors, put these vehicles out of the price range of the average motorist.

Plus, after years of very low cost driving with our old Leaf, the thought of going back to filling up at the same cost as diesel or petrol isn't particularly appealing either. That's if we could get hold of hydrogen. There are just 11 public access refuelling stations in the entire UK. Five are within the M25, there are just two in Scotland and none in Northern Ireland. Our nearest is two hours away.

In the last year, headlines have heralded the imminent conversion of millions of gas dependent homes to hydrogen, which would surely make refuelling more straightforward. But that's not so. I had always assumed the hydrogen all these futuristic vehicles used was produced by splitting water into its constituents via electrolysis, with the resulting electricity turning the wheels: green hydrogen.

It turns out the vast majority of commercially available hydrogen is produced through the cheapest option, steaming natural gas, which releases greenhouse gases. So, the overall result of driving a fuel cell EV *may* be a smaller carbon footprint for your mileage than you'd get hurtling around in a conventional motor. But it does feel a bit like we're back to square one on the hunt for emission-free transport until cleaner extraction methods can be scaled up.

While we wait, there are small but surprisingly effective ways to reduce carbon emissions in traditional combustion engine cars. They include turning off air conditioning a few minutes before the end of your journey, turning the engine off if you're idling for more than 10 seconds, changing gear and braking earlier, getting rid of the roof or bike rack to restore whatever aerodynamics your motor once had and even checking tyre pressures. Under-inflated tyres can reduce fuel efficiency by as much as 20%.

If you need a taxi, use pre-ordered cars rather than flagging one down. So-called ride hailing, with all that driving around looking for a fare, is 69% more polluting than the journeys they replace. [45]Yet again, it turns out the cheapest way to do something is also the greenest.

With all this going on before we even get onto the subject of air travel or shipping, it's no great surprise that transport is now the only sector where carbon emissions continue to rise.

Shipping accounts for 3% of global emissions, but without serious action that will rise to up to 130% of 2008 levels by 2050.[46] And yet the latest, strongest plan to do something about that has amounted to cutting just 1% of emissions over the coming decade by improving efficiency and banning the use of heavy fuel oil in Arctic waters. That's it.

Consumers were startled when coronavirus arrived and emptied the supermarket shelves. The phrase 'global supply chain' started popping up at the checkout. Emissions, and supporting our local community, are the big reasons why we buy everything, not just our food, as locally as possible, regardless of the fact that our purchases are already second-hand. Supply chain resilience is a bonus. It's clear that if we want any kind of environmental action on shipping emissions, we'll have to take the matter into our own small, but collectively powerful hands.

❊ ❊ ❊

Worldwide, greenhouse gas emissions rose by 25% between 1990 and 2010. Over the same period, emissions from international aviation and maritime transport jumped 70%.[47] Though almost equally culpable, there's no question that we're much more preoccupied by the battle over flight.

By 2019, aviation accounted for 3.5% of all human activities that contribute to climate change. In fact, so far it accounts for 1.5% of all the CO_2 ever produced. Half of that was produced in the last 20 years. Just before Covid struck there were one million people in the air at any one time. A city in the sky.

The world's airlines were carrying 4.5 billion people a year. But with only 5% of the world's population ever having been on an aircraft, it's clear that a very small number of people are taking most of the flights. In the UK, more than half the population never flies.[48]

The more exclusive, the lower the passenger numbers. The lower the passenger numbers the less efficient the mode of transport and the higher the individual's emissions. Those who turn left at the aircraft door into First Class or Business are, by doing so, emitting between two and four times the carbon dioxide per kilometre on their journey than someone sitting in Economy.[49]

Politicians, heads of state, business leaders and celebrities whose loud voices now increasingly ring with the problem of climate change, are, when they fly by private aircraft, responsible for between 20 and 40 times the emissions of an Economy passenger on a scheduled flight.[50]

We know that burning fossil fuels is an antiquated way of getting around these days and that, because of the demands on the engine, take off and landing are especially polluting. The easyJet era of £10 flights has been environmentally disastrous.

In 2018, the United Nations was projecting that international aviation would triple by 2050. But by the end of 2019, the International Council for Clean Transportation was warning that emissions were already growing 70% faster than the UN's forecast.'[51]

Unfortunately, carbon dioxide emissions, even though they hang around for hundreds of years, only tell around a third of the story. Astonishingly, the biggest contribution to global warming from aviation comes from the contrails or vapour trails – the clouds of ice crystals formed by aircraft engines at high altitude – because they reflect and trap escaping heat from the atmosphere.[52] It turns out that, when we add the effect of contrails into the carbon and other emissions produced by aircraft, scientists now suggest that flying is twice as bad for the environment as we previously thought.

So now we've got two huge issues. The first is that even the Paris Agreement on climate change only includes domestic aviation, there's no provision for international flights, which account for 64% of all air travel.

The second is that aviation's non-C02 effects are not covered by the former Kyoto Protocol in the same way as, say, methane from the agricultural sector. As things stand neither the contrails, aerosol-cloud effects nor release of greenhouse gases like nitrogen oxides are counted.[53]

The kids and I haven't flown anywhere since May 2017, just before Beanbag Day, and we don't plan to do so again. The truth is that I've got a lot of making up to do. I took my first long-haul flight at six weeks old. My parents' jobs and then my own mean I must have taken hundreds of flights by the time we decided enough was enough. I miss it a lot – from the endless possibilities of duty free and the feeling of being pushed into your seat as the runway falls away to the sudden change in smell and temperature as an aircraft door opens.

Being able to travel is a great privilege. If there was another way, and endless cash, I would jump at the chance to jet off with my family towards that never-ending horizon. I still want my children to see the whole world in all its glory. They just might have to get the train. Which, potentially, is good news all round.

In the roll call of carbon emissions by passenger kilometre, domestic flights come top of the infamous class. Petrol and then diesel car journeys are next, followed by short- and then long-haul flights. Slightly less polluting are buses, motorbikes, cars with a couple of passengers on board and then EVs charged through the National Grid.

At the bottom of the list, the least polluting are the UK's rail service, ferries if you're a foot passenger and finally, the Eurostar.

In terms of direct emissions, domestic flights cause 225ge of carbon dioxide per kilometre travelled by its passengers, and while the UK's freight train emissions are currently climbing, passenger emissions are down to 35ge.[54] The Eurostar emits just 6ge. If we were doing anything more than the school run, we would go by train.

The French train system, powered by nuclear electricity, has one of the lowest carbon footprints around[55] and we had just returned from a family holiday in the Pyrenees as Covid arrived in early 2020. It was a train journey we did with four under 5s, one heavily pregnant adult and another awaiting back surgery all over a week when the French rail system came to a standstill due to industrial action. It should have been a nightmare. It was brilliant.

My schoolgirl French improved no end as we tried to negotiate the passage of eight people across three countries on whatever trains were still running. But instead of stressing about the kids screaming in the narrow aisles at 25,000 feet, we watched the countryside roll by while they stretched out across the table with colouring and games.

It was a big adventure, a hit with the kids, and one that was significantly cheaper than flying. Plus, thankfully, the food was better. Local wine was involved too.

I've loved the train since I first entered the Agatha Christie world of the sleeper from Euston to Inverness in my early 20s. Dinner in London, breakfast at Aviemore, and a G&T in the bar before bed? Sign me up for surely the most civilised transport service known to man. And, yet again, it's often a cheaper option, especially if you're fast off the mark when they release new booking dates.

Earlier this year several European countries announced the reintroduction of their own overnight train services in a bid to counter the effects of short hop-on hop-off flights across our small continent. Sure, this isn't pure altruism – they had spotted a gap in the market as more and more people ditch flying, especially for single business meetings.

Sleeper trains are no longer the stuff of tweed suits and 1960s handbags, they are the future of travel. I cannot wait to tuck the kids into bed in Zurich and for them to wake up in Rome. Maybe they will get to see some of the world's wonders after all, without contributing to its destruction as much as I did.

But while train travel is certainly better than flying, it isn't completely emission-free. By acknowledging this but deciding that actually, we weren't prepared to give up travelling entirely, we had to acknowledge that we'd finally started to reach some, though not all, of our hard limits.

I had a feeling we would start coming up against those boundaries with increasing frequency too – and soon.

10. Widening the Net

By now it was two and a half years since a seemingly straight-forward decision had snowballed into a reassessment of pretty much everything we did. And by now the way we did those things had largely become automatic, normal, the way things were, the way they always would be. Everyday life was cheaper, healthier and, unexpectedly, simpler and calmer. We were on a roll. But we still had no idea whether any of this was actually doing any good.

We always knew that, ironically for a lifestyle which relied on diving into some complex numbers, we would have few quantifiable indicators with which to measure our progress. Then I stumbled across Earth Overshoot Day, a now infamous calculation that has been made every year since the 1980s by scientists desperate to distil the avalanche of complex data, models and theories passing before their eyes into one clear message.

Earth Overshoot Day picks out the hypothetical point in the calendar at which we have used up all the resources that the planet can regenerate in a year. It is the notional day that we start destroying more than we can sustain. When the calculation was first made in 1987 that date was 23rd October. We had overshot by more than two months. By 2019 though, that date had plummeted to 29th July. We were maxing out the world's biocapacity just over half way through the year. Somehow scarier though is the fact that the 2020 Earth Overshoot Day was 22nd August. The 2020 pandemic, with its all-stop across huge swathes of the world and its fundamental curtailment of many aspects of life, only bought us back three weeks.

It is worrying, but not exactly surprising. We all know where we are heading. I guess it is probably your motivation for reading this book. But we were surely doing better than that in our house, right? We'd changed so much, put so much effort into pulling everything apart and putting it back together in an environmentally friendlier way, we must have greatly lessened our impact.

Besides, the natural world certainly seems to recover fast, healing the wounds we inflict on it so quickly that in some places it is impossible to spot the disused quarries or abandoned settlements for the abundance of nature that colonises them. Just ask the weeds in our garden.

You can work out your own personal Earth Overshoot Day by inputting your info into an online calculator, so we did ours. I don't know what we were hoping for, but it wasn't the answer we got – the 4th January. It happens to be David's birthday.

To be clear, that's 4th January the following year. In other words we were hypothetically using 365 days' worth of resources over 369 days, which doesn't sound too bad at first.

But we had only bought the world back four days' worth of recovery. For all our efforts we were barely out of the deficit, barely breaking even. And we needed to do better than that. To have any sort of a future, we all have to help our environment recover, not simply stop it deteriorating any further.

Here was an independent, quantifiable, if reasonably basic assessment of our effort. And it has found us wanting. Were we still kidding ourselves then? Believing we had the faintest idea of better ways to do things, but actually having barely any effect? Had we been sucked in by the greenwashers after all, despite our best efforts?

Deflated, we sat back from the laptop and had a rethink. One answer kept coming up again and again. We had done plenty at home to change things. But only really at home. Only really in terms of our own little isolated space or, at most, actions we were directly responsible for.

Modern societies don't work like that though. We're not subsistence farmers with little interaction with the outside world. We rely fundamentally on other individuals, businesses and services to get by and they rely on us for custom, taxes, and votes.

It was time to expand our horizons, but we already had a bit of a head start. By 2020 we were starting to widen our responsibilities in small ways that we didn't really register at first because they seemed like such obvious and automatic extra steps.

We were regularly playing a game with the kids at the end of a day at the beach for example – the first person to pick up ten pieces of plastic gets to decide what we have for tea. The number of pieces goes up the older they get and no member of the party is exempt from the deal, even if they're not a blood relation. Sometimes a group outing in the school holidays can mean 20 people removing hundreds of pieces of plastic in a few minutes without really noticing.

We found ourselves joining organised clean-up groups along riverbanks and footpaths. We were picking up other people's rubbish from the hedgerows around us every time we went out for a walk – the sweet wrappers and plastic bottles that we then sent to a local charity to recycle for much needed cash. I even became that irritating woman who offered to collect up the crisp packets after kids' parties.

It is great to see how many charities are now embracing the possibilities of recycling for money. But I have no idea why the UK still doesn't have a European-style deposit scheme for throwaways. The queues for the bottle banks to recoup cold, hard cash at supermarkets on the Continent offer a powerful message about the ways we can quickly and easily alter consumer behaviour for the benefit of all.

Besides, we used to do it. Once upon a time, half the neighbourhood kids would scavenge glass bottles and return them to the corner shop on a Saturday morning in exchange for a few pennies that were immediately handed back for sugary treats. The whole thing appeals to my inner nine-year-old.

All this got us thinking about the services and facilities we rely on. Some we barely think about, others play a big part in life. You won't find us, for obvious reasons, spending thousands of pounds on exotic holidays, but we do love a decent pub, cafe, or even a grown-up restaurant if we can secure a babysitter.

Plastic straws and stirrers are now banned in restaurants and other hospitality businesses and most cafes or coffee shops knock a few pence off when you bring in your own mug. It's a reasonable start that nudges us into a reminder that our consumption doesn't begin and end at our own front doors. But away from a newly opened veg cafe, there weren't many places near us that ticked many of the boxes on what was by now quite a long list of must-haves.

Sure, we were ordering locally, seasonally and vegetally, and no, we hadn't visited a global fast food joint in years. But if we wanted to eat out within a 30 mile radius, the chances were high that we would still be handing over our cash to businesses that regularly sourced their ingredients from the other side of the world, made their money by flogging largely meat-based dishes and chucked out a whole heap of packaging and waste food at the end of a day. Unfortunately, that meant we were increasingly avoiding them as we tried to match up our approach at home with the more distanced but equally real impact of our consumption elsewhere.

Eating at the homes of friends and family was easy enough. They were used to us by now and were graciously saving the eye rolling and frustrated menu planning for when we were out of range.

But – especially when it came to paying for food – while I wasn't about to start rummaging in the bins out the back to check for packaging pile ups we did need to delve into the world of hospitality.

I love food and I love its social side. Few things are more pleasurable than spending a few hours over a meal with good company. But being a restaurateur looks like insanely hard work.

And yet some cafes, restaurants and bars have still managed to step up to the sustainability plate, not just by cutting back their meat or jumping on the seasonal and local bandwagon either.

Some of the restaurants, cafes, bars, pop-ups and food vans out there are plant-based, some are zero waste, a few are both. A couple of the posh ones even have their own farms to help reduce those food miles – always in Gloucestershire or Sussex for some reason. They proudly cite their 20 mile sourcing radius in pride of place on their menus. Others mention the anaerobic digesters they have out the back that convert the energy potential of food waste by breaking it down without oxygen to produce mostly methane that can then be used as an energy source. Which obviously had me pondering the Doc's Delorean again.

I found one restaurant that is all of the above and is even decked out with second-hand furniture fixtures and fittings too. Sadly, it's 160 miles away, and we already know how long it would take us to get there.

So we stick to independent places whose procurement, front of house, marketing, and customer services teams are all the same person – often the person cooking. It means we get real answers to questions about sources and resources rather than head office blandishments.

Zero waste restaurant

Anita-Clare Field, chef-patron of La Petite Bouchée in Witheridge, Devon, is undaunted by the controversy that can and does crop up as she tells customers how her zero-waste restaurant works. To keep waste, particularly food waste, to a minimum she takes all food orders a couple of days in advance, so she knows she won't be over ordering like most restaurants.

Diners are encouraged to take any leftovers away with them in compostable cardboard and paper containers or boxes that came in through the door with raw ingredients earlier. During Covid the team sent takeaway diners home with goodies in mushroom boxes and Field says that by the morning there would be a pile of them left by her back door to go through the cycle again.

While there is a small amount of plastic in the kitchen — there's no point pretending there isn't any, says Field — it is washed and reused continually.

Around 90% of the restaurant's ingredients are sourced from a 10 mile radius, most often from the restaurant team's own gardens and allotments. Leftover fruit and veg is pickled or fermented and leftover used cooking oil is decanted and handed over to a certified firm to produce biofuel.

The restaurant is also one of the few in the region to be a member of the Carbon Free Dining scheme, whereby each diner is offered a 99p surcharge that funds tree planting in acknowledgement of the carbon footprint of their meal.

'Food waste is a real bugbear of ours,' Field says. 'There's no excuse for it and we try very hard to use absolutely everything up. Our aim is that the fridges are empty at the end of the week. Any food that isn't used is given to neighbours. It helps us end the week having used a composting caddy and produced a single black bag of waste compared with the industrial bins a typical restaurant would fill in a week, or less.'

'The restaurant business just isn't set up for anything but plastic throwaways, usually because of health & safety and time restrictions,' she believes.

La Petite Bouchée in Devon, UK, takes orders in advance, to reduce waste

'If you've got a 200 cover restaurant you just don't have the time to address the piles of waste you're producing every day when your food comes vacuum packed from a huge supplier. We have to challenge restaurants, suppliers and manufacturers on plastic waste and over ordering because it isn't working at the moment.

'There is an increasing awareness of food waste in the industry though,' she says.

'Lots of chefs around today worked for the old masters who had a different mentality to resources and waste, but that is starting to fade out and a new awareness of environmental responsibility is coming through.'

Vegan restaurants are now popping up around our little town, even linking up with local farming cooperatives. For them, it keeps costs down and investment local while the customer doesn't stress about having to check the menu for food miles or seasonality. We've done that on a night out and it makes us terrible company.

With surveys now suggesting three in every four adult diners[56] want the carbon footprint of their meal to be displayed on the menu, those numbers are starting to appear in venues ranging from remote pubs in Cumbria to fast food chains at King's Cross. Progress is being made.

❊ ❊ ❊

Some independent hotels are going seriously green too. Many big chains seem to still be peddling the 'we're not going to wash your towels because it's better for the environment' line alone. But there's a new robustness to some of the green claims among smaller, independent hospitality businesses.

The industry, or at least some of it, appears to have finally realised that at the very least, more efficient use of renewable and low carbon resources saves them money. And not just when it comes to refreshing those towels.

I always used to be the person who popped the free toiletries in my bag on the way out of a room. There was something about the smell, the shape and size of the bottle, the hope of rekindling a flicker of luxury when I closed the door of my tired flat.

By 2020 we hadn't been using them at all for a while, let alone sweeping all the little bottles from the bathroom into the top of the bag on the way down to checkout, because of the plastic, palm oil and other unsettling ingredients.

We aren't availing ourselves of the tea or coffee sachets, the milk portions in mini plastic jugs or tubes, the branded pens or stationery either. In fact, with the kids in tow, we find it all a lot easier to plump for self catering or camping so we can control the waste we create (or don't), and reduce our overall impact away from home.

Holidays are a time to relax, take a load off and set aside everyday concerns for a while. When you find yourself turning communal lights off because you're worried about how the energy is sourced, you can be pretty sure that's not quite happening. When I started taking our own cleaning stuff away with us like a 50s sitcom housewife it was clear things were getting a bit ridiculous.

Just how far do you take all this out there in the real world, though? If the vegan restaurant has a bin do we storm out? If the hotel's sheets aren't organic cotton do we cancel our reservation? Where exactly should we decide our responsibilities end, because not only was this journey to zero slipping back towards joylessness, we were starting to revisit the fear that we'd never leave the house again because of a bunch of stupid rules.

We do a fair bit of eco due diligence on the places we stay, not least because according to some calculators a typical £150 monthly spend in the hospitality industry results in the equivalent of almost 0.7 tonnes of carbon a year per person.

A single overnight stay for a couple of people in a modest hotel, two meals out for the family at a pub or even a long weekend at a campsite each month create roughly the same levels of C02e as a return economy flight from London to New York.

Here then was the next of those limits. It turns out that we weren't prepared to never leave our home in the pursuit of climate change mitigation. But, just as we could reduce the impact of our travel, so too could we change the criteria we used when we got to our destination.

There were solar panels on the roof of the last hotel we stayed at. The toiletries were refills from a local producer though we still decided not to use them because of the ingredients, the vegan menu options outnumbered the meat dishes three to one, the bulk of their seasonally-focused food was sourced from within a 20 mile radius and their waste policy was aimed at zero.

Best of all this was a reasonably priced place in Cornwall full of real people, not an overpriced and intimidating hipster hotel in Shoreditch or a crumbly Home Counties pile with ironic animal busts and velvet sofas. Nor was it the only one we could have plumped for along that small stretch of rugged coastline either. Things are definitely looking up.

Real life and real budgets limit dreams of an endless social whirl and a different hotel every weekend, though. It was clear that trying to wipe off the greenwashed hue of the tourism and hospitality industry to get at the genuine eco leaders was still doing little to lessen environmental impact.

League of nations

As a nation, the UK doesn't have the worst carbon dioxide output per head of the population when it comes to fuel combustion. That dubious title is reserved for countries including Qatar, the UAE, Bahrain, Kuwait and Oman. These nations come in at more than 20 tonnes of carbon dioxide per person per year compared with a conservative global average of 4.4 tonnes, and their totals are rising by around 3% a year as of 2018.[93] But with such small populations their global effect is limited compared with the countries pumping out a lot of CO_2e by and on behalf of a lot of people – the US, Canada and Australia.

At the other end of the scale are some of the poorest countries in Sub-Saharan Africa, including Chad, Niger and the Central African Republic. It would take people in these nations a year to get through the average carbon emissions

---

your typical Australian or American would burn through in just over two days.

At the end of 2018 average UK emissions per person were a shade under 6 tonnes – somewhere in the middle and dropping by around 1% a year. That's in large part because a significant proportion of our energy nationally is now coming from nuclear and renewable sources. Last year was our greenest year on record as average carbon intensity – the measure of carbon dioxide emissions per unit of electricity consumed – reached a level not seen since the industrial revolution. Between 10th April and 16th June we didn't use any coal for energy production at all. It has all been counted as a massive win for a nation trying to present itself as the green leader of the world.

It all makes you wonder why, as I write, the first deep coal mine on British soil for 30 years is still in the planning pipeline, due to extract the stuff from underneath the Irish sea for use in the UK and European steel industry. Described by a local MP as an environmental disaster, campaigners argue the coal wouldn't be suitable for such a use anyway. But the government, which repeatedly talks about the risks of dithering and delaying over climate change action, chose not to intervene in the planning decision until the eleventh hour after huge public and international pressure. The go-ahead would have sent the rest of the world a deeply hypocritical message from a supposed climate world leader about the need to decarbonise industry and prevent prospective overseas mining projects . A public inquiry is now under way.

It also makes you think about what exactly the mix of energy coming through the wires into our homes is.

11. Green Energy

I had always naively believed that if you switched to a renewable energy supplier and tariff you would be home and dry on the green energy front. Even when I was digging down into the details of what different energy suppliers actually mean by 'green,' the structure of the National Grid never really occurred to me.

The contracts we sign with our various suppliers simply mean they throw power from a particular source into a reservoir of energy and we draw our share out to run our homes at the other end. A supplier injecting renewable energy into the grid sits alongside coal-powered power stations.

There are other problems too, especially when our suppliers don't generate or directly source the energy in the first place. In order to claim that all-important '100% renewable' stamp, the majority of the UK's energy suppliers buy Renewable Energy Guarantee of Origin or REGO certificates. These certificates are supposed to indicate what share of the energy coursing through our homes has come from renewable sources.

The UK regulator Ofgem hands out one certificate for every megawatt hour of renewable energy a company generates. Those certificates can then be sold on, alongside the power generated, or separately, to energy companies that then use them as proof to the regulator Ofgem that they have sourced their energy from renewable sources.

In other words, you could just buy the certificates – at an equivalent cost of only around £1.50 for each customer's energy use – and source the electricity from wherever you like, but still legally make the renewables claim. It's greenwashing.

What all this means is that unless you're generating your own electricity, a mix of green and traditionally sourced energy will be pulsing through your homes.

At the time of writing, the mix was around 2% from coal fired power er stations, 42% from gas fired power stations, 18% from nuclear energy, 29% from renewables including wind, solar and hydro, and the rest from 'other sources.'[57] Which basically means that despite paying for 100% renewable electricity, and UK electricity halving its carbon footprint in the last ten years[58], we still need to reduce our usage as much as possible. I'll admit these were things I'd been lax on until this point, under the illusion that our energy use – including when we plugged the car in at home – was guilt-free.

Throughout the journey to zero there have been instant fixes and slow burns. Our job now is to make our draughty home, full of Victorian single-glazed windows, as energy efficient as we can. This is one of those slow burns. Insulation is now rammed into every corner going, including under the floors and in the cracks around doors, but we're still saving up for new windows.

For now, though electricity sourced from renewable sources is often cheaper, we still try to refocus on reducing our energy consumption while we daydream about solar arrays. Lighting only rooms that have people in them, using LED bulbs, only boiling enough water in the kettle for our immediate needs, flicking appliances off at the wall and cramming as much as we can into the oven and fridge freezer saves us around £200 a year.

We are very aware that by processing and cooking everything from scratch at home we're missing out on the efficiencies of scale afforded to packaged food producers. Blitzing a handful of nuts in our home mixer means a far higher carbon footprint per home-made jar of spread than for every one spinning off the conveyors in a factory. So we try to cook and process in big batches to minimise our energy consumption and emissions. Lids go on pans and the fridge and freezer are kept as close to room temperature as is safe.

There's a quieter, bigger eco disaster haunting our home, though. Between 80 and 90% of the UK's homes are, like ours, connected to the gas grid. We are heating our homes by burning natural gas, a fossil fuel. Gas releases around half the carbon of coal. Nationally, our gas boilers are emitting the same C02e as petrol and diesel cars. Simply, we won't hit the UK's 2050 net zero target without drastic action on heating at home. 'The next five years are critical in deciding the future of heat in the UK,' we've been told[59] by those in the know. They warn that adequately reducing emissions from the UK's existing homes will depend on switching more than 20,000 properties to low-carbon heating every single week between 2025 and 2050. That is a massive requirement for which there is currently no adequate plan, despite public appetite for change. Meanwhile, plans to prevent new homes being fitted with gas boilers from 2025 have been quietly dropped.

All this means that our family – and, it seems, most of the country – should find workable alternatives. And that isn't easy. It turns out that open fires and wood burners are the biggest source of the most dangerous kind of air pollution – both inside the home and out. Their tiny particles get into the lungs and blood. It's the reason bags of coal piled up in petrol stations will, by law, soon be a thing of the past and why people are getting upset about burning wet wood in homes.

That left us bouncing between air and ground source heat pumps, solar panels, and forms of ultra insulation that might convert our draughty Victorian home into a passive house. Most of these solutions are complicated to retrofit, untested, or both. All require significant capital, even with a new UK government grant designed to bring the cost of heat pumps in line with traditional gas boilers.

While we work on that particular slow burn, we're only heating the rooms we use and wearing extra layers of clothing while in them. Friends remain much more enthusiastic about accepting invitations to ours in the summer than when a wintry draught blows their hair on the sofa.

We stubbornly hold out against whacking up the heating on the thermostat. Surely, sitting there in three pairs of socks in January and hoping for a lottery win to boost the window fund, we must have shaved that little bit more off our carbon footprint?

By 2020 the world wide web had many carbon calculators offering to quantify your personal impact on global warming. We took them all with a bit of a pinch of salt, acknowledging that they probably weren't taking our indirect emissions into account with any consistency. But even with all the breaks we could give ourselves, we were still sitting stubbornly at around seven tonnes of C02e a year compared with the national average of 13 tonnes.[60]

It was clear that changing our heating system and getting our home close to passive was the only way we would be able to stamp out any more meaningful chunks of our home's carbon emissions.

That was going to take more time. So what else could go while we saved and researched?

I never imagined that putting my foot through a beanbag would change our voting decisions, but the shift in our lifestyle choices has shifted our political views. A candidate or party that champions a genuinely robust environmental policy now gets a lot more of our attention – and we're not alone.

The environment and climate change was the fourth most important issue at the last UK general election. A fifth of the country considered it a top three concern along with Brexit and healthcare.

At the same time that the target to reach net zero as a nation by 2050 begins to make its presence felt at a grassroots level, eight in ten local councils in England and Wales have experienced climate-related incidents in the last five years. Nine in ten have now declared a climate emergency but they're still battling a lack of funding, legislation, regulation and sometimes even a decent grasp of their own carbon emissions.

12. A Bit More Zero

Apparently, recycling is a bit of a psychological con.

For starters, we tend to only recycle things we think have value. Hand someone a clean, smooth piece of paper, for example, and ask them to dispose of it and they will often plump for the recycling bin. Get them to cut it up first and studies into behavioural economics have found it is much more likely to go to landfill.[61]

At the same time, a takeaway coffee cup with your name on it – which behavioural scientists assert is psychologically then linked to your identity – is more likely to be set aside for recycling than one without. Apparently, you're not about to chuck out a piece of yourself.

It makes sense that we make the time and effort to deviate from the default route to landfill for things we deem valuable. Just think of the heavy, pure white box your last piece of tech arrived in. The one that made a rich 'shhhing' sound as it slowly revealed its contents. It might even have had a magnetic catch that snapped shut on you with a neat click. I bet you hesitated before putting it in the recycling or landfill bin. There are definitely boxes like that still tucked in drawers around our house full of useful stored things that have nothing to do with their original contents. We were firmly employing the golden rule of everything having a value, especially for storing crayons. Happy days.

But there's a problem. Behavioural scientists, who have spent a long time rummaging through university bins in Boston, have found that the positive emotions associated with recycling tend to obliterate negative sentiments around waste. In other words we use up a lot more of a resource if we know we can recycle afterwards – if we think our actions are guilt-free.[62] We have already decided we're going to do something positive so we let ourselves off the next not-so-great thing we do, like using masses of paper we don't really need in the first place because we've given ourselves a get-out-of-jail free card. This kind of psychological balancing even has a beautifully enigmatic name – 'moral licensing.'

Does that mean we are all wandering about stocking up on even more food covered in plastic because recycling is the answer? Maybe. The amount of plastic coming out of the nation's supermarkets is still going up, not down.

With the ban on plastic by now well established in our house, we had no way of knowing for sure. We were grappling with a slightly different question instead. With so much plastic already out there, already doing so much damage, were we scuppering attempts to clean up the planet because we refused even recycled plastic in all possible circumstances?

Should we be paying to give this throwaway material a new lease of life, a monetary value, a commodity to be hoarded not jettisoned? If plastic is already out there it surely makes more sense to re-use it? Yes, it does.

But after a while – and this remains a tricky call for us – we decided to stick to our stance on plastic in our home, largely because the last couple of years have shown us it doesn't need to be there anyway.

But the other point about all this is that recycling isn't the pana-cea we are all looking for. First off, it seems like a great place to hide. Apparently, you can recycle virtually anything these days, though it is not always easy, accessible, or reasonably priced – as we had found out with those polystyrene balls.

Simply stamping 'fully recyclable' on an otherwise entirely un-sustainable product is not a solution. In any case, that juice carton, (containing a product with a surprisingly high carbon footprint) is probably still on its way to landfill even if its design incorporates a green leaf.

We just don't have a good enough track record on recycling, whether that's because of psychology or practicality or both. In fact, the latest government data suggests household recycling rates have plateaued and are now even falling slightly, coming in at 45% of to-tal waste in 2018, despite the long-standing target of 50% by 2020.[63] Manufacturers know the majority of the waste they produce doesn't get anywhere close to the 'fully recyclable' claim they make.

Then there are those whose entire marketing campaign alludes to protecting the world's oceans because 10% of one of the compo-nents in an otherwise unsustainable product is ocean plastic. The other, bigger, problem is that plastic can't just go round and round the recycling loop forever. It degrades each time it goes round, which means that eventually you have to start adding in 'virgin' or newly created plastic into the mix.

In a bid to work out which approach would do the least damage and make the most positive difference in our house, I had found myself going through reams of research about what proportion of global plastics recycling uses what process and whether plastic-eat-ing enzymes may or may not save the planet any time soon.

That, finally, led to the uncomfortable question of where and even if recycling happens at all.

We absolutely should recycle rather than bin things. We all

know that. Our four year old knows that. The problem is that even if we get over all these monumental logistical hurdles and can categorically say we have recycled something after we used it that doesn't get us back to zero.

Though recycling offers a massive saving on materials and C02e emissions compared with throwing them into landfill and starting again, collecting, sorting, transporting and processing them for recycling does use energy and generate carbon.

By now our recycling bin hadn't seen plastic for years, but there was some metal and glass. These don't degrade like plastic, so can be recycled almost infinitely as long as they aren't contaminated.[64]

We started with glass, which consisted mostly of wine bottles. It emerged as a far bigger problem than we had realised. The chance of your bottle of plonk coming in virgin glass is surprisingly high. Unfortunately, the UK's glass recycling isn't quite where it needs to be. Green wine glass found in the UK contains around 68% recycled glass.[65] So there's still 32%, in a perfect process, to go. And that's the best number out there by far. In 2016, just 30% of amber glass and 32% of clear glass was included in 'new' glass products in the UK.[66]

Then there's the impact of transporting something that heavy, weirdly shaped and fragile, even if it is cheekily bottled only once it has been shipped to our shores in large plastic containers.

Although we were sticking to our organic, local, English or western European food and drink sourcing criteria – which delightfully offers a delicious range of options on the vino front – we couldn't get away from the fact that this still wasn't that great for sustainability. A huge proportion of the carbon footprint of our tipple of choice – wine, which can come in at 2 kilograms of C02e per bottle,[67] is down to the packaging and its impact rather than the contents themselves.

It wasn't looking good on the booze front.

International incidents

As I've mentioned, in 2018, just 45% of UK household waste was recycled.[94] For starters, that means we're recycling less than we were just a few years ago, which was news to me. [95]I'd assumed we were on an ever-upward trajectory. But the latest numbers suggest we won't even have met the basic Europe-wide target of 50% by 2020.

There is good news though, we're smashing it out of the park when it comes to cutting landfill waste. Though we're still dumping 7.2 million tonnes of waste into these vast pits and mounds every year, that's actually only 20% of the amount that went into them in the mid 1990s.

Sadly, that's probably because so much more of our waste is now incinerated. In fact, the headline figures suggest we're burning as much as we are recycling. The amount of waste we torched rose from just 15% in the mid 2000s to more than 40% just 15 years later. The number of incinerators in the UK has doubled with plans for far more, despite the implications for air pollution and carbon emissions.

Defenders of such an approach point to heat and energy generation through the Energy from Waste initiative and dispute some of the claims made about the risks to health from living nearby. But is this really the best solution we can come up with for waste that could otherwise, after reprocessing, be a valuable commodity? Even advocates acknowledge that incineration is last on the list of options after reducing and recycling.

It seems we're burning our waste because we can't ship it overseas anymore. Two thirds of our waste has traditionally gone to China, which banned imported plastic, paper and textile waste at the beginning of 2018 amid concerns over hazardous contamination.

So then we diverted more of it to Malaysia, which introduced its own ban at the end of 2018 after being inundated with waste. By 2019 Malaysia's officials were publicly calling out nations including the UK for foisting plastic and other recyclables onto developing countries already facing huge problems.

Leonid Danilov, Pexels

By that stage we were sending increasing quantities to nations like Indonesia and Turkey. And yet Indonesia's own waste management and recycling systems are failing to process 90% of their own material, to the extent that so much unprocessed waste ends up in rivers and lakes that the country is regularly cited as one of the worst marine polluters on the planet.[96] How much of those apocalyptic rivers of plastic heading unrelentingly out to sea in fact originate from UK households? The truth is, we don't know.

In fact, nobody seems to know. In 2018, the National Audit Office warned: 'The system appears to have evolved into a comfortable way for government to meet targets without facing up to the underlying recycling issues.'[97]

There are no real assessments of the effectiveness of the current system and few checks I could find about what eventually happens to the waste. With the most recent figures available stating that half of all packaging recycling is sent abroad,[98] it appears impossible to find out exactly how much of the recycling we put out in those little green boxes on a Thursday morning is properly processed – either domestically or overseas – and how much just adds to overall pollution.

Every few weeks there seems to be another story of British waste being sent back to us by nations that, for example, find used nappies and sanitary products in waste exports labelled as paper. This is deeply disturbing stuff that goes way beyond the usual complaints over which local authorities recycle what materials and why the hell they can't all be the same.

Nobody seems to be in much of a rush to sort this out. Deadlines to reform the current system in England,[99] including the introduction of deposit schemes and a joined up approach to recycling across local authorities, have now been pushed back until the end of the current Parliament, which could mean nothing changes until 2024.

Meanwhile, an investigation by the BBC in 2020 found vast swathes of British-origin plastic and other 'recycling' simply dumped and burned by roadsides in southern Turkey.

Campaigners continue to push for far more transparency and comprehensive guarantees over the waste chain that stretches from our shores across the globe – guarantees that many argue we won't ever get while we continue to dump our waste and recycling problems elsewhere.

With so many uncertainties in the system the only conclusion we keep coming back to is that mass recycling is not the answer to our wastefulness as a society. The inconvenient but simple truth, as far as we can tell, is that we have to turn off the tap at its source.

On to the next thing in the green box. We've never been big consumers of aluminium drinks cans but what about the tins? UK consumers buy food in tins that are usually steel coated in tin. Only 25% is recycled material. Which means 75% is virgin. Unfortunately the steel industry is one of the highest carbon emitting industries in the world. Steel production and imports to the UK alone are responsible for around 26m tonnes of carbon emissions every year.[68]

Until the UK fully embraces the economic and environmental benefits of embracing recycled steel – which are considerable, including for the beleaguered domestic steel industry – and those steel cans and glass bottles are closer to 100% recycled, it is clear recycling needs to be a resolutely last resort, not a get-out clause.

The mantra we were taught as kids – and which I will forever associate with Eddie Izzard thanks to a noughties TV campaign – is reduce, reuse, repair, recycle. In that order. We were sticking to that, if only for our own sanity.

Anyway, I would welcome the opportunity to avoid the recycling centre as much as possible. It's a miserable place. I want to dive in and yank all that still useful, still valuable, sometimes even very beautiful stuff out. And judging by all the sad peering over the edge as their items smash to smithereens, plenty of other people feel the same way.

I have a slightly unhealthy obsession with the BBC's *Money for Nothing*, a TV show which rescues items in the split second before they are hurled into the recycling centre skip and employs master craftspeople to reinvent them before selling them on at some eye-watering prices.

Every time the original owner is asked if they are willing to part with their things for regeneration rather than being tossed, the answer – regardless of the person's background, income bracket or environmental engagement – is always something like: 'I didn't think there was still a use for it,' 'I didn't know what else to do with it,' and 'I'm so pleased it isn't going to waste.'

By the beginning of 2020 the next big push in our house was entirely unavoidable: it was time to cut out the recycling. Luckily we had no idea what we'd let ourselves in for, otherwise we probably wouldn't have started.

We had always tried to grow a few veggies ourselves but it had always been a bit half hearted. We even had an allotment once but that only lasted a year before the retired custodians of the surrounding plots complained about the nettles. Even after going zero waste we were saved by veg boxes and the local greengrocer.

This was going to be the biggest change to our eating habits. The zero recycling decision would turn us into what Americans would call 'homesteaders.' It was good timing, taking much of the stress out of food shopping during the first wave of the Covid-19 outbreak.

It started well.

The temptation was to try to grow all sorts of weird and wonderful veg. But we knew from a quick audit of the last round of tins that what we really needed to start with were sweetcorn and tomatoes. A lot of tomatoes. Chopped ones, whole ones and above all that rusty-coloured sauce to go over beans. Beans were temporarily a point of fervent discussion too, not least because we had been eating them for decades but had no clue what kind of beans were baked. Haricot, as it turns out.

Meanwhile, we learned how to make the few items we still bought in glass, quickly discovering that, just like the pre-made foods that had once arrived in our house in plastic, most of these automatic purchases were stupidly easy to make at home and usually tasted better. I'm still annoyed about being hoodwinked over mustard.

Inevitably then, the first weekend of the March lockdown was spent sowing tomato seeds in a propagator we fashioned from a weird collection of things we found around the house. The kids got involved with the lettuce and herbs.

In preparation for what would surely be an enormous array of prize-winning produce, we made a raised bed in the back garden out of planks from an old agricultural shed that had collapsed. David became interested in the no dig method of plot maintenance.

Being outdoors so much energised us. We planted more trees, the kids put together some decidedly unattractive bug hotels, discussions over locations for mini-ponds began in earnest and we set aside a third of the garden to grow wild.

The lawn, once mown monthly, now gets a haircut twice a year. We have also planted other types of grass and plants to boost the biodiversity. Best of all we had an excuse not to do the weeding – it offers much needed winter cover for minibeasts, apparently. Walking through waist high grass in midsummer now sends up clouds of insects.

We sowed and watered, and watched things actually start to grow through the warm spring and early summer of 2020. After all, there wasn't much else to do by that point in the pandemic.

We had made a point of buying food in season, usually to mitigate the carbon footprint of hothouses and long-distance trucking. I can't help thinking in-season food tastes better too, but it had always somehow been a side show, a small component of wider living. Now seasonality was looming large. As was crop failure.

We never would have imagined that tomato blight would cast such a big shadow over a summer. Or that the sight of torrential rain smashing down maize that had only recently been convinced to grow at all would be felt so keenly.

The freezer had taken on new significance when we switched to zero waste and I'd had dreams of freezer drawers full of sweetcorn that would brighten up a dreary February lunchtime. It was now clear to me that, irritatingly, there wouldn't be a single kernel to set aside.

The prospect of the hunger gap made its presence felt in our lives like never before. While we wouldn't actually allow ourselves to go hungry – that's extreme, even for us – we needed to bridge that gap by preserving the food that was abundant for three months to live off for the rest of the year. We started planning for winter like a scene in a low budget apocalypse movie.

In the midst of all this I remember catching a documentary about a surge in the number of 'preppers' out there – the people organising themselves for the end of days. Some of it was worryingly familiar. When the lead interviewee started talking about 'taking it to the next level' by making his own bread I had to switch over to *First Dates*. We were miles past that point by now.

Our kitchen had become a mini processing plant. Ironically, we found ourselves sliding towards some of the preoccupations with efficiency and value that can lead to exactly the kind of unsustainable resource and ingredient use in the commercial operations we avoided.

Dry food turned up in reinforced paper sacks. Really big ones that I couldn't lift. Jam happened. We had a go at marmalade. Bottling became a thing and I searched, in vain, for a second-hand pressure cooker that would be big enough to deal with a conveyor belt of pasta sauce, vegetable soup and plums in 'light' syrup. We had failed to understand quite how much sugar we suddenly needed to make it taste like the canned fruit we used to buy – a great deal as it turned out.

We pressed and bottled apple juice from the old neglected tree in the corner, while others (why are there so many cooking apples in the world?) were dried in slivered rings or wrapped up in newspaper and stored. We even made our own vinegar, though that was by accident.

There were food sources from elsewhere to acknowledge and explore in a new light, too. We had always ambled along the odd hedgerow vaguely on the look-out for blackberries to gobble on the hoof but in late summer 2020 we developed a full-on foraging strategy. We went picking in earnest.

We follow the rules of not stripping everything you see and staggering your take, but we had every intention of raiding the long forgotten cherry, plum and damson trees around the local school and factory with the hope of filling the freezer. We came home several evenings on the trot with stained fingers and full bags. Or rather the adults did. The children rolled through the front door with stained everything and full stomachs, which wasn't the point of the exercise, but they didn't care.

After a slightly disastrous first summer, those ruby jewels went straight into the freezer and helped plug some gaps in what even we could see was going to be an inadequate winter supply of vitamins, minerals, colour and, quite possibly, flavour.

More remarkable was how enthusiastic everyone else was about all this. Maybe it was because of the bizarre, home-based year we all experienced in common. People we barely knew went out of their way to hand over their gluts and pass on bubbles of long-cherished insight into everything from where to find a forgotten walnut tree to cautionary tales about the importance of sterilising. Day after day that autumn our neighbours lined apples so perfect they were cartoon-like along our wall to be included in the general master plan.

That plan started to mean the lead time on food prep had gone from a few minutes pre-Beanbag Day to a few hours after zero waste kicked in, and was now approaching months as we started setting aside and storing. As the world continued its crazy trajectory outside we suddenly had food security the likes of which I had never known before. I guess there are people out there who have a huge bunker full of tins and bottled water. But we've never really had much in our cupboards before. I hadn't expected a shift to zero recycling to be so... reassuring in some quiet, backed-up, old-school way.

Our daughter renamed the kitchen cupboard 'The Store Stump' after the communal larder in the book *Brambly Hedge*. Which was maybe a bit twee and mouse-ridden (the book, not our cupboards), but I knew what she meant.

With a new respect for seasonality I found myself occasionally lost in old snippets of information about heritage ingredients and antiquated recipes, rhymes, songs and wisdoms, too. Some of them even worked. We took part in our town's apple day; there's wassailing, too, here in January, with high levels of cider consumption. It's easy to take the mickey out of this. But as Covid-19 heaved its way through the population and the world became a wobblier, sometimes frightening place to be, we felt like we were focusing on something that felt a bit more stable, real, tangible, and positive than daily death figures and family tragedy.

It wasn't just us either. Far from it. As the security of global supply chains faltered, the pace and breadth of modern life was forcefully curbed and the state of our mental health was acknowledged like never before, we Brits hit the garden centres and cookery books in a big way. For a while we weren't the only people buying their bread flour in 25kg sacks. There was sudden, slightly aggressive interest in our sourdough starter. It dawned on us that we were doing the same things as everyone else for once. It was really nice.

By the autumn the most unlikely people in our lives were bringing us reused jars full of delicious homegrown, homemade concoctions. Preserves were discussed by our younger, trendier friends without a hint of irony. 2020 was terrible for so many reasons, but it was a year in which we felt included, part of a tribe in a way we hadn't for a while.

Finally, miracle of miracles, a local food store started a fill-your-own wine bottle service. We'd already lucked out with the proximity of cider and ale breweries whose refill schemes had started somewhere in the 1930s and never quite gone away, but now we could do this zero recycling thing. And crucially, we didn't need to move to a smallholding to do it.

Then the rose tinted glasses slipped. All that bottled and jarred veg patch produce that I'd smugly lined up on shelves with the absolute conviction that it would see us through a nuclear holocaust didn't even get us to the end of the year. The freezer was emptied of smooth tomato marbles by the 1st February and the apples so carefully wrapped according to strict instructions had turned to a sweet mush – and not in a good way. We still don't know why.

The sauerkraut was a disaster, too. I had been so pleased with myself that the sudden influx of cabbage was going to be transformed into something delicious that also aided gut health. (It may be the first thing you learn in Fermenting 101, but it's remarkably tricky if you don't use cling film.)

We had vastly underestimated pretty much everything from the quantities and time involved to the appetites of deceptively small children and some of the small but, we now realise, crucial details involved in preserving food. We acknowledged our failures as the tins reappeared in our cupboards again last winter, though fewer than before. Their carcasses will probably necessitate a green bin on the pavement every once in a while until the summer.

The downshift to zero recycling, we were realising, wasn't ever going to be a quick win in the same way that zero waste had been. We have so much to learn, so much to understand. A long, slow rhythm to get into. There's a reason the allotment champions around here are mature. It takes a while to take on the wisdom necessary to battle that blight.

That doesn't mean we've given up. No way. We are now armed with a grand total of two year's experience with which to charge into a new growing season.

David has been talking about converting the frame of an old trampoline into a polytunnel that will be the answer to our short growing season prayers and – big news – there's an unlikely looking log hanging out in a damp corner that I'm assured is going to provide us with mushrooms. 'Impregnated dowels' are involved.

So now, despite our resistance, we seemed to be sliding helplessly towards the 's' words – self-sufficiency. But while we forged ahead some of the changes we thought were long put to bed threatened to re-emerge while we weren't concentrating.

13. Ghost in the Machine

There's something weird about all these throwaways, synthetic fibres, palm oil and unwanted chemicals. They seem to occupy such an integral place in our 21st Century world that if you turn your attention elsewhere for a second, they return. Lose concentration for a second and a biro will suddenly appear out of thin air. Even after several years of going zero we still have to reassert the basics occasionally.

Keeping out all those furtive materials was also causing some hefty life admin. We would call and email the producers of everything we bought to find out how the product would be packaged. If we couldn't pick up something in person, we would implore every online auction or marketplace seller to send us the things we needed in an old cardboard box or reused paper envelope rather than a plastic post bag.

For every online order, we spend an extra few minutes checking that parcels aren't about to arrive on our doorstep in acres of bubble wrap or peanuts (remember those?). We decline the freebies pressed on us in the street and even the synthetic toy membership gifts included in the welcome packs sent by the most environmentally fastidious of charities.

Rather than recycling reams of pointless printing after the resources have been used up and the ridiculously heavy results trucked around the country, we try to cut it off at the pass.

We were already aiming to be a paperless home. We don't take receipts for purchases, refuse flyers and handouts, and appeal to those approaching our letterbox not to leave 'unsolicited mail' as if we were channelling Hyacinth Bucket.

We don't buy physical newspapers or magazines, we use the local library and we have spent years working through every company that once sent us physical letters and catalogues explaining that we need their contact by email or not at all. We signed up to the Royal Mail's door to door opt out scheme that now halts most of the remaining strays.

Paper-free applies to everything, from our private life to work documents. The children's paper use is harder, with all the artwork and exercise books, but homeschooling during the pandemic gave us more control over it, and a series of alternative options and behaviours to pursue. We have always encouraged the children to use scraps of old and pre-used paper to create their art masterpieces.

With less and less paper in the house that wasn't really working any more so we picked up a second-hand electronic writing tablet. They love it, and it means physical handwriting and drawing hasn't halted. They still earnestly grip the 'pencil' with little fingers, practise forming letters by 'sliding around the snake' with their tongues stuck out in concentration, and run over to proudly show us their latest drawings. This is surely what their future 'paper' use will look like. But, if I'm honest, something about the swap is a bit unsettling and I can't quite pinpoint why.

A general shift away from real paper is worth it. We knew the widespread use of paper bags had been such an environmental problem that they prompted the development of the plastic bag. But we hadn't realised that getting a single catalogue or magazine that then gets chucked away creates the same carbon footprint over its lifetime as a litre of cow's milk. Even recycled, a couple of weekend newspapers every Sunday produce the same emissions over a year as a flight from London to Barcelona.[69] Working from home for the UK's only all-digital national newspaper, I thought I'd dodged a bullet for a while there.

But we couldn't get away from the fact that everything and every action has a carbon footprint. Everything has an impact. As living mammals, we know zero impact is ultimately impossible. But it was clear there was still room for improvement when it came to inconspicuous consumption.

We found ourselves wondering about all the virtual work, school, entertainment and other activities we were doing online. Was there a way, we wondered, of reducing its impact? Ideally, without becoming crap at our jobs overnight or straying into agoraphobia?

Most of the carbon footprint for the technology-based, web-dependent work and leisure we do comes from the production of our devices. And though plenty of the stats out there about the impact of our tech use tend to leave out those calculations, we prefer the whole picture.

Roughly, the bigger the device the bigger the footprint, so we've stayed small on purpose, sticking with a very domestic sized TV and we don't bother with desktop PCs.

We were aware of the massive problem of e-waste, the impact of leaching metals and the health threat to those who deal with it in unregulated environments, especially children. But just extending the life of a single computer and monitor from four to six years can take out 190kg of CO_2e[70] too, while doubling the life of a phone halves its carbon footprint, so we're going to cart our old faithful laptops and battered mobiles around for a while yet.

Our virtual consumption has an impact too, albeit a fairly minute one compared with, say, a long weekend in Miami. In some ways it's not really the tool you have for the job, it's the way you use it that counts.

The most polluting way to watch terrestrial TV for an hour is on a big old 55-inch LED TV. It produces roughly the equivalent C02e over a year as driving 500 miles in a combustion engine car.[71]

Even in 2019 each UK adult was already watching just under five hours of audiovisual content – from watching an actual TV to streaming on our phones. By April 2020 being stuck at home increased that by an average of an hour and a half per person per day.[72] And how many of us give the telly our sole attention anymore either? I'm not sure I remember the last time I watched anything without also scrolling on my phone.

Globally, our gadgets, the internet and support systems account for 4% of carbon emissions – and rising. With stark warnings over the 'blind transition to an… environmentally unaudited digital world,'[73] we started delving into these behaviours.

We are enthusiastically reassured by every silicon valley giant that their operations are greener than green, that their energy is renewable, every business breath and data centre flicker is covered by carbon offsetting and sedum adorns every available inch of roof space everywhere.

But that's not the case consistently across the world. Some people will definitely be able to calculate that but if you're anything like me you won't have a hope of working out where exactly your online actions are dealt with or how much impact your everyday actions have – not only in carbon emissions but also on water and land use.

Internet use in general, globally, has an equivalent carbon footprint that can range from under 30 to more than 60g C02e, as well as using up to a third of a litre of water, per gigabyte (GB). [74]

With a GB allowing us to, for example, watch a couple of hours of standard definition TV, read 1,000 emails or browse the web for just under a full day, the typical mobile user was using around 4GB a month on their phone by 2020. And that was rising by almost 40% year-on-year.

Clearly, what we do with our remarkable connectivity makes all the difference. Streaming in high definition on a phone, which incurs a carbon footprint eight times larger than that of standard definition – doesn't happen in our house anymore. In fact, the Royal Society is now appealing to streaming services to make standard quality their default to help tackle climate change.

Elsewhere it turns out we can use the rock-solid 'I'm reducing my carbon-emissions' excuse for turning the video function off on Zoom during meetings and family quiz nights that have persisted beyond lockdown. This single action could cut out almost all of the 1kg carbon count of an hour long meeting as well as around three gallons of water.[75]

Not all apps are created equal though and while services like WhatsApp and Facebook are at the lower end of the C02e, land and water footprint for each hour's use, Netflix, for example, remains startlingly high across all three, not least because of that high definition problem. I trained myself out of the habit of having it on in the background sharpish.

Then there was the work stuff. We've all had the 'Please consider the environment before printing this email' statement obediently pasted into our email signatures for years now. But like three quarters of the UK we had no idea of the carbon cost of our inboxes. One study from 2019 suggested that we send 64 million unnecessary emails every day – messages that often contain single words: 'thanks,' 'cheers,' 'great,' 'LOL' and others.[76]

But while it is always important to say thank you, the argument was that if we could cut these unnecessary unactionable notes out, we could save tonnes of carbon, not to mention quite a lot of collective time. If every British email user sent one fewer email a day, we could reputedly save 16,433 tonnes of carbon a year – the same as 81,152 flights to Madrid or taking 3,334 diesel cars off the road.

But the truth, when you break it down, is that an email's footprint depends on how long it takes to write and read. The longer the email, and the greater the number and size of attachments like photos, the more electronic activity required in production, processing, transmission and action by the recipient at the other end. Cutting out your single, average sized email will actually save far less than 1g of CO_2e.

So we aren't going to save the planet any time soon if we're doing it one email at a time, and experts quite rightly suggest we all focus our efforts on the big stuff that makes a far bigger difference first, starting with flying and meat consumption. But we already had those in our sights, and it was increasingly clear that all these lifestyle changes are much more impactful if they are based on applying a different attitude to our resources overall. At its core, a more environmentally aware lifestyle came down to recognising essential value and treating the resources we used with an acknowledgement of that value. It was about not wasting anything, however intangible, however insignificant it seemed. So we started sending fewer emails.

Tweaking some of these habits and behaviours would barely register with my personal annual carbon footprint but it did make me rethink my liberal use of the out-of-office. That and the 42,000 unopened emails hibernating in my inbox. I obviously do still say thank you at the bottom of a longer email, and I'm proud of the fact that us Brits really do express our gratitude more than any other nation, but I do now resist the temptation to get caught up in the endless 'No, thank *you*' electronic exchanges.

Unsubscribing from databases online with as much commitment as we were with paper mailings in the real world also helped steer us away from the 'ooh look, there's a sale on, I'll just have a quick look...' browsing rabbit hole that somehow ends with a surreal afternoon walking tetchy Alpacas in Shropshire drizzle before you can say '60% off days out.'

There's more good news too. A decade ago those whose job it is to worry about this kind of thing warned that as our reliance on the internet exploded the energy required to support such activity would become unwieldy to say the least. But that hasn't happened.

The energy demands of the world's data centres – the physical buildings full of a company's computer networking and server systems – account for just under 1% of all the energy consumed everywhere in the world.[77] Despite a 60% increase in demand over that 10 year period, the energy consumed has remained surprisingly flat thanks to improvements in processor efficiency and a drop in idle power.

So far, diving into the world of intangible services had been about lowering our impact. The global conversation and co-ordinated action – at least as far as we can see – is focused on not making things any worse. But that isn't going to get us out of this mess. Only regeneration can do that.

So we found a search engine that worked just like the world's most famous service but bought and planted trees instead of rewarding shareholders. Now the designated search engine for all our connected devices, Ecosia takes the money it earns from advertising revenue and sets aside 80%, almost half its total revenue, to plant trees from the UK to Madagascar, the USA and Brazil to Australia. By the time of writing, it had planted 137 million.

On a basic level, we had been successfully stripping our financial support from businesses that would sell environmentally destructive goods and services for a while now – even down to those purchases we couldn't see and barely registered. We had examined the primary layer of products and services whose delivery into our hands had an environmental impact and reduced or removed them as far as we could go.

Now being able to start adding a new, more upbeat layer of these small, free, easy switches into the mix definitely helped us to feel like we were in a good place. It was a psychological ledge on the lifelong climb where we could catch our breath.

But our little family unit could still pack a much bigger punch than the tiny carbon footprint coming off the odd bit of Friday afternoon email banter. In fact, the potential impact from changing our relationship with our next target was so huge that failing to address it would have made a mockery of everything else we had done so far.

The sheer scale of it meant that if we got it right, we could make a massive dent in four tonnes of C02e we produced every single year – more than half of our annual carbon footprint – because of the attitudes of companies almost all of us engage with every day of our lives.

Unfortunately, untangling ourselves from their tentacle-like omnipresence wasn't going to be quick or simple.

14. Follow the Money

One of the last of those infuriating plastic-windowed envelopes to drop through the letterbox confirmed that I had closed a bank account. We were in the middle of the weird Covid spring of 2020, when there was more time to address the tasks we had all been putting off for ages. By now we had worked our way through most of our products and services and severed links with those that weren't pulling their environmental weight.

Only our relationship with the financial services industry and its wholly inaccurate insistence that secure contact can only be achieved through post, continued to be a physical, doormat-landing problem. That wasn't a great surprise, though. After all, financial services posed the biggest environmental problem of all. And yet this is rarely mentioned in the sustainable living chat.

We can go on about zero waste, the bid for zero recycling and the ban on flying and meat until the cows come home, but if our cash is still held in financial institutions that invest it destructively, we are deceiving ourselves. A whopping half of the average UK consumer's footprint comes not from the penchant for a long-haul hot holiday or the siren-like allure of a bacon sarnie, but from the impact of our financial affairs. And if the matter of who does what with our wealth has the biggest effect on our personal environmental impact, that also makes it our greatest weapon in the eco battle.

As a financial journalist, I had convinced myself that I was on top of it all. Certainly, everything we'd done with our money in the last few years had been rooted in sustainability criteria that sought not just to lessen our damage but also to support change-makers.

But as I tapped out more and more stories about the ways the world's biggest banks, insurers and fund managers were still ploughing cash into some of the most polluting industries known to man, I started to get twitchy, especially about aspects of our financial lives buried so deep under the demands of everyday life that most of us have forgotten about them.

So while we were grappling with the basics of industrial hydrogen production and tomato growing, we had also been spending the previous year going through all our money, finding out exactly where it was, what it was used for and how we felt about that. We set about it in the same way we had pulled apart, examined and then reconstructed everything else. It made for some uncomfortable reading.

When we set up savings accounts for the children they were opened with an ethical bank whose green credentials even extended to plant-based debit cards rather than plastic ones. With the bank only investing in businesses wholly engaged in environmentally positive actions and outcomes – like carbon capture, storage technologies and renewable energy – the kids' accumulated birthday and Christmas money is pretty green. We're as confident as we can be that their cash is not just doing as little harm as possible, it is funding environmental regeneration. Unfortunately, we couldn't be as confident about the grown ups'.

For starters we realised we still had an old bank account with Barclays. In the years since the Paris agreement was signed in 2015, Barclays and HSBC have collectively invested £149bn in oil, gas, coal, tar sands and fracking. At the last count, that put them on a list as the worst banks in Europe for financing climate change, [78]and yet somehow they still claim to be aiming for net zero by 2050 (despite Barclays investing more in fossil fuels in 2019 than it did in 2018).

That Barclays account was jettisoned pretty quickly, but some financial relationships had to be ended rather than moved so we sat tight and paid them off as fast as possible. Luckily, the mortgage was already with an ethical building society.

In terms of general, everyday money management, that only really left our insurance policies. Insurers have a vested interest in curbing the damaging consequences of climate change, such as flooding. Climate change will cost the world's insurers trillions of US dollars according to global accounting firm EY, but on the whole they are moving woefully slowly.

Some UK household names didn't even bother to reference environmental, social or governance criteria in their business strategies until 2020. It turned out that our home insurer was one of the most uninterested so we trawled some of the environmental affairs platforms that now offer comparison site-like league tables for a better solution.

And because these firms wield some hefty investment clout of their own, I also dug into how our choice had voted on climate-related matters as an institutional investor in some of the world's largest businesses. It checked out there too, but many don't. Too often insurers and many other large businesses will state their commitment to protecting and regenerating the environment as a business, only to vote down similar plans as an investor.

When I came up for air, the switch had halved our annual premiums. So buoyed up by a triple tick in the box, we took a deep breath and turned our attention to more complicated stuff.

There are three ways to financially back a company – buying its products or services, investing in it directly yourself, typically by purchasing a share of the business, or putting your money into a fund along with lots of other people's money that then invests in that company and others.

Most of us go for options one, or three, or both – unless you've got a lot of time and cash to invest in stocks – which we don't. But when it comes to finding a green home for your cash it seems to be getting harder as the world embraces climate change action, not easier.

For a while, the big problem with ethical, or socially responsible investing was that it was so niche and based so entirely on deciding the kind of companies and activities you wanted to avoid that nobody really expected to make much, if any, money with these criteria in play. These were options for philanthropists, not real people. Now, the problem isn't that this approach is a niche loss-maker, it's the opposite. Everyone wants in, and with good reason.

In 2020, figures from the UK's Investment Association showed the amount of cash going into responsible investments had quadrupled compared with the year before. By then, the majority of ethical, or as they are now known, environmental, social and governance (ESG) funds had outperformed their conventional counterparts over the previous decade, which means the die-hard green investors are now being joined by those who simply want a good investment return.

These days, the questions being asked about ESG investing aren't whether this approach is becoming mainstream, they're about how soon the world of investing will stop being based on anything else. Deloitte predicts that as soon as 2025 half of all professionally managed funds will be environmental, social and governance ones.[79]

Whether you're what's known as an institutional investor making decisions about where to invest the collective pension savings of thousands of people, or a retail investor – someone like you or me trying to find a good home for a bit of extra cash – the environmental credentials of those choices are now critical.

Around the world, coronavirus was a tragedy. But it also supercharged a sustainable investing trend that was already well under way. As the first wave of the virus flew around the world between April and June, more than US$71 billion went into ESG-style investments[80]. In the UK, more money was invested this way between April and July alone than had been in the previous five years combined.[81]

For some, the social, community and societal part of ESG criteria had suddenly come to the fore, while others became acutely aware of global supply chains, their impact and fragility, for example.

Whatever your motivation, it all boils down to one thing. Follow the cash and it now seems to lead to all things green, whether you're a tiny business bringing innovative carbon capture technology to market or a commodities leviathan that has realised it is increasingly difficult to flog oil and gas in an anti-emissions world and is now trying (and largely failing) to convince shareholders it has been 'beyond' fossil fuels for years.[82]

The big money has finally turned up to the eco party because investors will lose out if they stay on the pavement outside. And with big money comes big business and big politics.

Four people in a random zero waste household somewhere in south west England are not going to change the world, particularly when the two shortest ones don't have many voting rights. A thousand people on a Friday school strike won't either – not by themselves. But money like that will.

When hedge fund managers start backing Extinction Rebellion, as at least one has, it's OK to start believing we can turn things around. But with the world tripping over itself to highlight its eco credentials, there's now a different problem facing those of us without a lifetime of investment analysis – greenwashing on an epic scale. If every business out there is trying to convince us they are leading the eco charge, how are we supposed to work out which ones really are?

What about the umbrella-like funds that invest in a range of companies on our behalf and create, by their very nature, extra distance between us and the impact of our money?

This seems like a nice problem to have if you're lucky. But it actually affects most of the UK population because 80% of UK employees are now enrolled in a workplace pension scheme, setting aside a small proportion of their salary every year, which is then topped up by both their employer and the government. It is the biggest savings pot the vast majority of us will ever have. Pension funds take that money and invest it in a series of funds. Unsurprisingly, these are the biggest investors.

Not only are millions of people building up savings pots they haven't ever had before, but the money we now hold in those investments is also the most powerful weapon most of us have in our ecological arsenal.

Most people don't get much say in the way their workplace pension is invested – at best getting a handful of approaches to select from. And although there should be an ethical option among them, nine out of ten people are still in the default fund chosen by the administrator. Needless to say I flung yellowing paperwork around until I was reassured that our various tiny retirement pots were as green as I could make them.

High-profile campaign groups like Make My Money Matter are now shining a bright and unwavering light on the environmental opportunities for these vast pots of money. The new Pension Schemes Act 2021 will force larger occupational schemes to report their exposure to climate-related risks and opportunities annually to members and the public. It's a starting point. We can only hope the continued pressure, including strongly worded letters from belligerent savers like us, will help shift these vast sums away from the highly destructive industries they have been bankrolling for decades.

Where should we put our money instead?

More than 500 sustainable funds launched in Europe alone in 2020.[83] The problem is that there are still few universal standards or measures over what constitutes a sustainable fund. The European Commission did launch a green-list of sustainable economic activities in late 2020 to help private investors identify genuinely environmentally sustainable businesses based on emissions thresholds and categories such as climate change mitigation, water and marine resources, and waste prevention. While it has been criticised by those industries that didn't make the cut, such as gas power plants, concerns have been raised about the inclusion of businesses that burn wood for energy or generate hydropower, because of their impact on local ecosystems. More importantly, this European scheme isn't universal and countries, including the UK and Canada, are now developing similar tools. Unfortunately they are being developed for expert and professional investors rather than ordinary citizens.

So if any of us were lucky enough to emerge from the chaos of 2020 with any extra cash to invest, where do we start?

The way businesses that we invest our money with deal with the question of environmental responsibility isn't really that different from businesses that you buy anything else from. Just like out here in the real world – in the supermarket aisle and the shoppers' website – 'eco-friendly' covers a disconcerting range of criteria at a variety of depths.

You could, for example, go for a fund that only invests in clean energy companies providing electricity from renewable sources and exploring new technologies. Seems fairly straightforward so far, but putting your money into leading edge innovation can be risky.

Then there are the funds that invest in companies which have upped their game on the ESG front. How do you feel about those? Because they will still seem terribly discerning at first glance but could include some companies that have only changed their ways because their arms have been twisted. Indeed, you may find you are investing in some bog standard, environmentally dismissive businesses whose credentials have improved only in line with the law in their home nation.

Indeed ESG simply means a fund that works to some level of environmental, social and/or governance criteria. In other words they could ignore the environmental side completely and appear at the top of various league tables because their track record on investing in companies with strong governance is good. You can quickly find that pure-as-the-driven-snow ESG investment includes everything from oil and gas companies to car manufacturers.

In other aspects of life, when we reach information overload we retreat to the fundamental three questions. Managing our money was no different. It just took a bit longer to unravel than the grocery shop.

Luckily, at least for this exercise, we didn't have huge, complicated investment portfolios or, as you might have already guessed, vast payouts or dividends propping up the bank balance. That was important because fossil fuels have historically been some of the biggest sources of income from investments, which makes them tough to walk away from, regardless of whether you're an individual investor or a fund manager trying to deliver for your clients.

Free of the ponderous issues that come with great wealth, we took what scraps of money we had in a couple of funds and examined their investments, moving our cash away, or divesting from the kinds of businesses and business practices we avoid in 'real life.'

Even that pretty clear, 'dark green' approach isn't without its controversy, and there's an argument for remaining invested to lobby for change. Your average multinational oil company can throw a lot of money at new, clean technology.

But we'd rather invest in a fund that works with the businesses developing solutions rather than those still degrading the planet – even if it is at a slower rate. We actively look for funds that only invest in businesses fully engaged in climate solutions. Like the rest of the investing world, we're also increasingly interested in green bonds that raise money specifically ring-fenced for projects that deliver environmental benefits.

We'll have to keep an eye on changes to the couple of funds we've chosen, but we're at least now in a position where we're not blindly supporting polluting businesses and might even benefit from the green boom firmly underway in the investment world.

But what about that boom? That whole assumption of growth, of gain, that underpins that world? The one thing that has really got us into this massive mess is the constant, unceasing demand for more. More stuff for less money, more food from more places resulting in more waste. If there's anything that sums up the reasons for our relentless destruction of our environment, it is our endless appetite for more.

Going zero has become as much about not buying as it has about buying, about not pursuing more simply for the sake of having more. But that's a tough idea to get away from as we had already found out, not least because our entire economic system is based on growth. If a country isn't growing as measured by Gross Domestic Product or GDP, it is considered weak. A stable GDP is a problem.

But growth into what? And how can a nation have a robust economy if its natural resources are being decimated? That doesn't sound like a nation with a strong future to me, it sounds like a nation without a future.

If the biosphere is finite, why isn't the global economy? The world our economies rely on doesn't have endless resources. There's a limit to what we can extract, produce, burn, eat and consume and we've already significantly exceeded it, as we already know, every year since the 1980s. Some estimates suggest that the amount of stuff we produced per person doubled across the world between 1992 and 2014. But over that same period of time the stock of natural resources per person fell by almost 40%.[84]

To lay people like us this all sounds like we're blowing up a balloon of an economy inside a glass jar planet. The balloon may not pop first but the glass is surely going to shatter with the pressure any second now and then it's only a matter of time until the balloon explodes – probably not very much time. The cracks appeared decades ago but we're blowing harder and harder all the time. It's enough to make you shield your eyes.

Natural capital

The enduring, and alarming problem with traditional ways of measuring a country's economic health is that 'the progress and regress of nations do not recognise humanity's dependence on nature.'[100] Gross domestic product (GDP), the measure most of us recognise, is basically a big tot up of the value of all the goods and services created within a specific geographical area over a specific time period. It is used to gauge how well or badly a nation or region is faring compared with other periods in its history or other nations or regions.

And yet this economic gauge, this health check, doesn't look at the foundation of that capital for any clues about its strength. Which is nonsense. Natural capital, the world's stock of natural assets like timber, concrete, oil, gas and cotton is necessary to produce the clothes, houses, roads, energy, food, oxygen and water that sustain humans.

Without nature there is no life so there is definitely no economy.

If you're not taking nature into consideration when you measure economic status, how on earth can you know that an economy is strong or weak, growing or shrinking?

The forest versus the factory scenario is a good illustration of the problem. Build a mega factory by chopping down a forest and your GDP rises when you pump out the factory's products. But you've got no record of what natural capital you've lost to build the factory. And further down the line when the pollinators that once lived among those trees no longer reach farms that are now struggling with soil erosion from all that clearance, the economy will suffer.

Include natural capital in our economic models and not only will we understand the impact of our actions better, but we are also more likely to recognise the fact that permanent environmental compromise leads to permanent economic compromise. It's like a massive game of Jenga. Compromise the base layers and your whole structure comes tumbling down. Maybe not today, maybe not tomorrow, but soon.

So the fact that '...economic and finance ministries and international organisations today graft particular features of Nature, such as the global climate, onto their models as and when the need arises, but otherwise continue to assume the biosphere to be external to the human economy,'[101] is disturbing. And, frankly, from the outside looking in, a bit stupid.

Measuring natural capital or, perhaps more pertinently at this stage in the game, quantifying its depletion isn't exactly easy. But there is, hopefully, change afoot thanks to a clever blueprint for how to do this.

The UK Dasgupta Review – the first request of a full assessment of the economic importance of the natural world by a national finance ministry – has now come up with new ways of working that could change the game if they are adopted fast.

But they're not easy changes. GDP as a form of national accounting needs to be replaced by one that considers the depletion of natural capital. And we need an overarching international organisation that protects global public assets like rainforests, oceans. And poorer countries should be paid to protect ecosystems, and charges should be levied on those using international waters, to help protect fish stocks and other marine life.

The measure that chimes most with me is a recommendation that nature becomes a key part of educational curricula in a bid to shorten the distance – physical or psychological – between people and the natural world.

Now these proposals just have to be implemented. Everywhere and quickly. I guess all we can do is hope the world's politicians and diplomats can take a step back from their usual short-term preoccupations and make it happen.

15. Meeting Ourselves Coming Back

For a problem that threatens us all so fundamentally, our response to the climate crisis is weirdly personal. There is no correct or clear approach to dealing with it and precious little agreement on what is necessary or possible. One person's best effort is another person's greenwashing. Someone's deep commitment to the cause is seen as unworkable by their neighbour.

It is a big part of the reason, I suspect, that you should never discuss this in the pub – it won't end well. You only end up traipsing home tetchy, wondering why you spent the only child-free night out this month arguing with your mates. We've all been there over one subject or another.

We never seem to agree about what needs to change as a group of otherwise like-minded friends in the local, let alone when that debate is scaled up to national representatives at global meetings who are confronted by many other pressures and interests, too. But it turns out we don't even need to leave our house to find points of difference.

Other couples fight about the washing up, who rolls out of bed at dawn on Saturday to take the kids to gymnastics and where they spend Christmas. Don't get me wrong, we have some spectacular 'discussions' about those things too. But we also disagree about climate change.

More specifically, we argue in the patches of no-man's land between our individual approaches, behaviours and commitments, and in particular we argue about David's work.

We both love what we do. We're incredibly lucky. We do the jobs we said we wanted 'when we grow up.' So there wasn't really an issue about those roles until we started going zero.

As a journalist, primarily for a digital newspaper, my career is fairly environmentally benign. I work from home and I don't travel to meetings: they now take place remotely. The publication I work for has a strong and long-standing position on environmental protection, reflecting its readership's priorities.

David spends most of his time working on his family's organic farm, where he is regenerating the land, water and habitat. As well as doing away with all pesticides, fertilizers and fungicides, he has stopped ploughing and turning over the soil – actions which threaten to release carbon by breaking down soil structure and speeding the march of the world's exhausted farmland towards desertification.

Livestock are sparser and managed in a way that ensures they stay outside for longer, ideally all year round in a bid to remove the farm's dependence on oil and plastic. Meadows are now left on their own for months on end, hedgerows are being reinstated and existing ones left to grow out, all of which support natural regeneration and carbon capture. In the coming year, more than 100,000 trees will be planted on the farm to bolster the existing patches of woodland.

It's exciting, life-affirming, and a huge privilege to be able to join a growing number of farmers around the world trying to protect and regenerate the habitat that sustains us all.

But a few days a year he changes out of his mud-splattered hoodie and wellies and puts on the uniform of a motorsport engineer. He disappears to the other side of the country, sometimes the other side of the continent and directs carbon-emitting vehicles around in circles as fast as they can go.

Over the last few years I have lost count of the number of times we have unpacked this contradiction, tipped it up and pushed its jigsaw pieces around in a bid to find agreement.

The work offers our family an important source of income as well as a series of intangible benefits missing from isolated rural jobs, such as social contact. David is expert at the role. And while he remains as committed as ever to our zero approach in all other respects and does everything he can to mitigate the impact of taking part, for instance carsharing if he can't use public transport and offsetting the carbon footprint of his journey, that doesn't alter the bigger picture.

Motorsport, like other industries, is very slowly acknowledging its environmental responsibility. In the US, Nascar even has a carbon-neutral race team, whose certification relies on both emissions reductions and, inevitably, offsets.

Formula e, the EV version of all this, is gaining traction slowly, but is still a long way from having relevant opportunities for David, And besides, the cars themselves are only a tiny part of the problem. The long and short of it is that David isn't prepared to give up his work in the motor racing industry, undeniably damaging though it is. I entirely understand his reasons for sticking with it and I'd like to think I respect them. I just don't agree. It's a problem we haven't yet overcome.

In fact, David's decision to continue on as before in this small aspect of our former lives threw me completely.

For years we had been moving forward – fast, uncompromising and united. It had been exhilarating, and hugely positive in so many ways and I didn't want that to end.

But I guess we all have to draw a line in the sand somewhere, on everything. We reach a point that we're not willing to go beyond.

Perhaps it is because of a sense of risk, of jeopardising too much personal safety, security, disposable income, health or happiness. Even the world's most committed environmentalists have boundaries. They have to. We all do.

David had drawn his line. I thought, and still feel we had more wriggle room yet, that there was still plenty we could do. At the time I didn't believe I'd reached any of those limits yet. But I was wrong.

I wasn't ever going to stop my children going to school for the sake of the planet, or revert to some sort of Flintstone-esque tech-free lifestyle. I wasn't about to commit to never travelling anywhere again for that matter. But at no stage had I anticipated that one of the hardest decisions we had to make would be where to stop, when to say 'Enough now, we've gone as far as we can' about one or more aspects of life, however small.

Obviously, there has to be a slowdown somewhere on this journey because we all have an impact on the planet by virtue of the very fact that we exist. Every species will affect their environment. It's just that everything balances out if you have a well-functioning ecosystem.

All of which points to two things. First, we need to remember (and this is something we need to get better at in our house) that regeneration plays a crucial role. It's not just about reducing, cutting back, restricting. It's about putting the good stuff back in, replenishing the natural capital if at all possible. Sometimes nature can't burst back into life on its own.

Second though, we will never be able to resolve the question of whether we go far enough to protect our environment. Arguably, we could always do more in some way. We could all reduce our impact further. But that way lies madness and, if you take it to its conclusion, you very quickly end up living in a muddy hole only eating and drinking whatever happens to drop into your mouth. Or not existing at all. No thanks. We've got stuff to do.

Carbon controversy

Few ideas have as terrible a reputation as carbon offsetting. It is not helped by the fact that it allows CEOs and their army of marketing execs to claim the oxymoron of a carbon neutral airline or a global hub airport, to name but one industry that has sought to capitalise on the great offsetting opportunity.

Others include food producers and retailers, such as those dealing in fast food heavy on the meat and dairy items, global logistics firms and individuals from pop stars to presidents. And that's just the small stuff. Olympic games and even entire nations are now offsetting their carbon footprint. But is a carbon offsetting certificate worth anything at all?

Historically, when cash was often dropped willy nilly into an unregulated industry, the answer was: probably not.

Carbon offsetting has been around since the 1970s and essentially means calculating the amount of carbon emissions and other greenhouse gases produced by an individual or activity before taking the equivalent out of the atmosphere somewhere else by another means. 'The environment doesn't care where you take the carbon out' advocates say.

We often take that to mean forestry and tree planting projects, but in the past these have sometimes been deeply problematic. Some have prompted thousands of people to be evicted from their homes to make way for plantations, while in others, planted saplings have been abandoned and died. More still have used non-native species that cause problems among native habitats. Plus, if you plant trees they have to stay there long term — a tall order.

Other options include renewables projects, particularly

solar and wind power projects that help remove our dependence on fossil fuels and are often considered a more robust option. Elsewhere, certifiers offer methane capture projects on a far away rubbish dump or improving the efficiency of cooking stoves.

The once wild west nature of carbon offsetting is becoming tighter with better accountability and traceability. However, as massive amounts of money flow in thanks to compulsory business obligations as well as voluntary offsetting there are still significant issues. For individuals trying to do the right thing, these range from that tricky but now familiar question around how exactly you calculate your emissions through how you go about selecting the right project from a sea of options to whether those projects are verified. In general though, verification standards are much higher in Europe than in the US.

Essentially, you can still pay whatever you like to support any kind of vaguely relevant project, which fills few people with confidence. But if this is something you want to do, look for verified emissions reduction (VER) credits as a starting point.

Then there are the costs. Most voluntary offsetting setups are not-for-profit, but even these slim organisations still require as much as a fifth of the money to cover their running costs.

Instead of buying from a certifier, you could go down the DIY option – which is regularly cited as the best solution – after simply reducing your emissions, that is – even if you don't get any quantifiable credits. This involves calculating your emissions and then contributing to organisations or projects with a good chance of reducing carbon emissions through their actions. You could still choose to directly back

> a project like those offered by certifiers or you could take a different approach by funding a campaign to change the law, for example.
>
> Regardless of whether you're convinced by the process or credentials of these projects or not, carbon offsetting is supposed to be a short-term administrative stop gap while we work on fundamentally reducing our carbon emissions in real life. It is not supposed to be a paperwork confessional that delivers us, squinting but reassured, into the light.

I realised we were approaching such a point when I announced to the family one morning in lockdown three that I might have a go at making soap. The unanimous response, along with three faces showing complete bewilderment, was 'Why on earth would you want to do that?'

They had a point.

We are lucky. We have soap by our sink that adheres to the zero approach and we can afford to buy more when we need it. It was time to start giving ourselves a break, but I was uncomfortable about that idea. I didn't want to slow this down just yet and I couldn't work out why. After all, we had come so far and changed so much, there were fewer and fewer big plunges to take short of moving to an off-grid yurt. Maybe we were all reaching our personal stop signs then, or at least a few of them.

Going zero is a strange process. At least it is for us. At its most obscure, it has, and still is, making us re-evaluate concepts and attitudes so deeply ingrained and taken for granted that we had never imagined they would even be up for discussion.

What quantifies success, the interplay between family or cultural conformity and self determination, how we reward our children, what compromise means to us and whether that judgement is accurate or reasonable. These questions and so many others have come up time and time again as we try to grapple with what, it turns out, has become something of a new way of thinking, as well as a new way of living.

Sadly, there's no blueprint. There isn't one for any lifestyle. I wish to God there were. It would have come in very handy indeed.

From Beanbag Day forward, we have always tried to make decisions based on the most objective information we could get our hands on. That's why these pages have far more references to academic papers than anything else.

But before you can start running towards new goals, you have to plan your routes towards them. With such an enormous, all-encompassing subject, you have to come up with a deeply personal set of criteria to help you sift through a bombardment of information – and sometimes misinformation – to find the path that works for you.

If you can be clear about your criteria and own that plan, it will make it easier to prioritise action, what to set to one side to come back to at a later date, and what to jettison because there's just no more headspace available and you now need to go and sit down in a dark room with a gin.

We hadn't done any of that. We'd just jumped into a pool we couldn't see the other side of and started swimming. Now, because of that, we were starting to meet ourselves coming back round to some of the decisions we thought we'd made and put down. Some of them were big too.

All along, our priorities were to limit, and if at all possible, reverse the environmental impact of our modern lives. The social responsibility angle of ethical consumption was second on that priority list, if only for the sake of decision-making simplicity.

Often those two themes dovetail without much extra head-scratching on our part. The organic this or recycled that is often Fairtrade too, for example – the shorthand description of a relationship that works on a basis of fair business dealings, pay, working conditions. The bank that invests in reforestation also lobbies to outlaw child labour, backs education programmes, supports sanitation projects and protects women's rights. But sometimes they didn't tick all those boxes. The products we bought and services we used and the strategies we adopted weren't really taking the human dimension into account at all. It took us too long to understand that to ignore one side of responsible consumption is to undermine the other.

When I was little I believed people were the problem. After all they (my nine year old self didn't get as far as 'we') were the ones doing all the burning and polluting and chopping down and over-eating and hunting. Look after the environment, I figured, and all the people would be better off eventually, too.

My primary school brain never arrived at the fact that those people with more immediate needs may not be able to step back from excruciating and unrelenting pressure on their money, time, welfare and security to make changes that, in the short-term at least, only increase that pressure.

By the time I was living in one of the most expensive cities in the world in my early twenties with rent gobbling up all but £8 a week from my less than minimum wage income, the environmental impact of my consuming decisions weren't at the top of my priorities.

The cruel reality of all this is also that the people hit the hardest by the effects of climate change and pollution are among the poorest. In so many ways, environmental justice is social justice, whether you're in Indonesia or Ilford. Climate action cannot simply be a cause for the middle classes, because allowing that to happen will ultimately guarantee we fail.

It was high time we gave ourselves a shake and revisited some of the decisions we had made and the strategies we used, to acknowledge that truth. We went back and looked again at the food and other goods and services we bought, changing our choices to better acknowledge the human impact of our consumption. At least this time around we knew the drill.

Four years in, this wasn't the only revision though.

More recently we've adopted apps that inform us when local people and businesses are about to throw away food and other products. It sounds ideal, a very cheap, if not entirely free way of feeding the family with what regularly turns out to be excellent food. The first time we picked up such a bag of items it was full of perfect fruit and veg.

Except that they often come in plastic or are sourced from the other side of the world. Few are all plant-based, plenty are grown using pesticides and fertilisers. Cue another rethink. Is it more important to save food from landfill than adhere unwaveringly to our plastic ban? Maybe not. At least maybe not in every single circumstance.

This is not a linear or finite process. It took me a ridiculously long time to realise that was a good thing – a vital part of going zero. So now, while still learning new things and creating new plans, we also go back and change others. Maybe now it's just with a bit more ownership of that process and an unexpected sense of identity.

We have never belonged to a tribe. We like lots of things, go to lots of places and get involved in lots of events, but we had never been so encased by something so much bigger than us before. Certainly, not something we felt we could do something about.

We aren't religious, so there's no tribe or identifiers there. We're politically active. We vote on manifestos and love a meaty debate as much as the next person, but we're not members of any political party. We've attended a couple of demonstrations in our lives but aside from the school strikes for climate, they were mostly years ago before life intervened.

We enjoy music and went to a few festivals before Covid struck, but never felt compelled to be the first person at the barriers days before the main act appeared. Nor do we know all the words to every song by our favourite artists.

Sports are the same. We're certainly up for spending a wet weekend in front of the football or Six Nations, and even made it to a few events at the London Olympics during that remarkable feel-good summer that now, as we come to the end of lockdown three, seems like a lifetime ago. But we don't follow particular teams or have encyclopedic knowledge of any line ups.

We're not high followers of fashion or culture, and though I love delving into ideas and travelling, we haven't spent the last 20 years backpacking around the world.

We're happy and lucky and ambitious and try to make the most of our lives. We're pretty ordinary people though, maybe even slightly nondescript sometimes. But going zero has given us something substantial to believe in, an identity, a cohesion. Maybe that's why I was nervous about the compromises and rethinks and slowdowns that had started to come to the surface by the end of 2020. Maybe I was worried that we'd lose that sense of identity if we took our foot off the gas or changed our stance.

I needn't have bothered engaging in such navel-gazing though, because it's now clear this process won't ever be over. And nor should it be.

But the last four years have taught us a lot about how we can move forward better informed and with a real sense of what we could achieve. We know too, that when things get mind-bendingly complicated we can fall back on the three questions we started with:

- Where has it come from
- What will we do with it
- Where will it go

We will always need to revisit ideas and decisions and change things here and there, especially as new, better ways of doing things and new kinds of products are emerging as the world turns its head and sees the environmental freight train bearing down on us.

And anyway, not only was there plenty to still get our teeth into, our biggest test was yet to come.

16. House on Fire

We were starting to get somewhere. The pieces were fitting together and our pursuit of a better lifestyle, for us, our environment and the planet had solid foundations thanks to the last four years. Or should that be the first four years.

The once stressful agonising over every decision, every purchase, every behaviour and even the indirect impacts of our 21st Century lives had eased.

We had got over the initial panic of trying to work through absolutely everything in a dash to slash our impact. We were starting to feel like we could continue more gradually. Maybe we could bite off bits from the remaining challenges that we could actually chew.

There were plenty left too. We have agreed we won't get another dog whenever our pirate of a spaniel passes away. With such a meat-heavy diet, not having even a small dog could cut our annual carbon footprint as much as taking a gas-guzzling SUV off the road. Elsewhere there were still those damned windows to fit.

Small, easy wins were still coming to the surface too. A few months ago I had a proper forehead-slapping moment when I went to send a friend flowers. Per £1 spent, out-of-season cut flowers have one of the highest carbon footprints of any consumer good we buy[85] so we now make a point of buying native, seasonal plants instead.

Consuming ethically no longer means we have to accept second-rate customer service or products either. A once very limited list of goods, services and businesses that were robustly green was expanding rapidly.

We were enjoying less compromise and more freedom than at any point since Beanbag Day. Behaviours and restrictions that we established years ago could now sometimes be unwound, though not the big things. We're still waiting on guilt-free flight for example. That might take a while and even then I doubt we'll decide to jet off into the sunset without a care in the world. And all that lab-grown premium steak won't trickle down to us for some time either, plastic wrapped or not.

But other things were coming to us, often as a result of other people and other businesses doing things differently. Covid, for instance, prompted an accomplished home cook in a village near us to quit her day job to launch a vegan takeaway business. We filled rotating sets of metal containers with delicacies you just don't get around here – like vegan sushi or Ghanaian curry. She's now rolling out that service to all her customers. She is one woman in one small settlement. But there are other people like her everywhere. This grassroots force is coming to the surface across the world. Plus, thank the gods, takeaways are once again a thing in our house.

Either our lifestyle is starting to resemble that of more people around us or the other way around. I don't care which, I just know that every day the journey to zero is getting easier, not harder.

I'll admit, some of the things we've altered and the actions we've taken in the last four years have been hard work, frustrating and confusing. But like any changes any of us make in life they are only really tricky for a short time before they bed in and become business as usual, before they stop being a big deal and shuffle into the background.

Some have been very easy to make – a brief review of an assumed behaviour that makes a difference somewhere in the chain but has little or no discernible impact on us. Sometimes the smallest action has made the biggest difference, too, especially when it is to waste nothing or to take no action at all, to take a break from the consumption conveyor belt.

Going zero has been and continues to be a very positive experience – a surprisingly permissive one for a lifestyle that, from the outside, must appear very restrictive. Part of that liberation has been financial – which may surprise some.

Environmental awareness is handcuffed to an enduring perception of privilege. And if you walk into a zero waste shop with no context to go on I can entirely see why shelves full of pricey reusable versions of cheap throwaways would put you right off.

It seems that everywhere you turn eco equals expensive. But these items are simply the most visible manifestation of something much bigger than an opportunist making a few quid on a pack of stainless steel straws.

Our household spend is significantly less than before Beanbag Day. Our food bill is down just under 40% a month, for example, even with the organic premium, because we don't buy ready made foods that come with a margin for the middle men. Meat and dairy products are expensive, and rightly so. Without those on the list we've saved a fortune, even when adding in more nuts and seeds.

Our cleaning ingredients cost pennies where they used to be pounds, and slowing down the buying process on everything else has made a big impact too. A 'do we really need this, can we use something else or borrow it instead' fire break in the psychology of purchasing has been transformative.

If we ever thought about it much, we presumed the impact of this shift would be entirely physical. But the greatest effect has been psychological. We think differently about pretty much everything now, we approach new experiences and ideas and consider physical items from a completely different angle. I'd like to think we have a new appreciation of what goes into the products and services we use, that everything has value and that nothing should be wasted.

Going zero began because of physical items – the need to change things, not buy certain things, to sometimes buy other things instead. But it is now clear that everything stems from an underlying mentality of carefulness. Care around how we source things we need, how we use what we have and how we treat and respect resources – from food and energy to time and effort, our own and other people's.

Maybe I'm just quickly approaching middle age, but there are few things that are as quietly satisfying as smuggling the leftover scraps from making oat milk into a new meal or even just leaving the oven door open to use the residual heat to warm the room.

We reuse everything from building bricks to baking parchment. Last week I got a smug satisfaction out of cutting up a snapped belt to make a handle for the dustpan and brush. If we can only get one round of use out of something it's now a bit of a fail. It's fun and free and the kids love the creative possibilities.

These are definitely the kind of things my grandparents would have done. That circle is positive too. As a nation we've lost touch with these, and other naturally conserving behaviours and norms. Elderly people gleefully recall racing the neighbourhood children round street corners to collect up abandoned glass beer and 'pop' bottles to fund their sweet stash. Our grannies and grandads, aunts and uncles knew what it was to consume calmly, carefully and with dignity within the scope and boundaries of their lives, confident in the true value of the relatively few items they surrounded themselves with.

I only wish I had paid more attention during the school holidays when they talked me through the shelves of already ancient but immaculate tools that lined the shed. They are long gone now – the sheds, the tools and the people. But I have found myself thinking of them increasingly during these first four years.

When we started taking the 'we need to change our lifestyles' message seriously we didn't really think about what that would end up looking or feeling like. We thought we would be looking endlessly forward, but frequently we've found ourselves borrowing from the past.

Completely separate aspects of life have started to join up and hold together. We're slimmer, and healthier personally, but so is our home. It is less cluttered and easier to clean, tidy and organise. That makes finding things easier, which in turn makes the daily 'where's my other shoe' conversation when we're already late for school less common.

Even TV watching seems to follow a theme.

Every TV documentary, every interview, every article from every corner of our global village – from the densest of biological research to the fluffiest of lifestyle blogs seems to point in one direction to one underlying truth – that we are overreaching ourselves in every way, everywhere. Rein it in, dial it down, take a breath, they all scream, and we might yet get ourselves out of this mess. Check back in with the difference between need and want, between right and privilege and there's still hope.

If there has been one takeaway from the last four years, that's it.

By summer 2020 we were riding high, buoyed by everything from fewer aircraft making ominous vapour trails over our heads as the result of Covid, to a healthier bank balance, smaller waistlines and now regular requests for eco tips from friends and family.

It seemed like we were surviving lockdown just like everyone else without our zero approach causing us to starve, too. That was a big deal: a leap forward in confirming the validity and robustness of this new life.

For some time we had been wondering if we could keep this up no matter what. The pandemic seemed a good test and we were getting by with few real issues – aside from buying jeans. People around us were even defaulting to some of the same behaviours. It was all going OK.

And then in the middle of this global crisis David went for what we assumed was a routine blood test. He came home with a diagnosis of incurable leukaemia.

My strong as an ox, former international sportsman of a husband who had never smoked, barely drank alcohol and ran and cycled kilometre after kilometre every week had a cancer that usually affected people twice his age.

He was, and still is, remarkably sanguine about it. I fell apart, hiding it from him so as not to increase his stress, which I had read could make everything worse. Nevertheless, I started down the classic journey of shock, despondency and anger at the same time as trying to research a way out of membership to a club I hoped none of us would ever join.

Because of my family history, I always thought of cancers as lumps and bumps, tumours in specific areas of the body. Clear, identifiable, with defined boundaries that show up on the scans all ready to be cut out and, please god, banished.

Leukaemia is often linked to external factors, such as industrial chemicals – pesticides, insecticides, weedkillers. Like the ones used in the fields around David's family home.

There's a reason some nations call leukaemia 'the farmer's disease.'[86] Last year, the owners of the weedkiller RoundUp, widely used across farms, parks and gardens, agreed to pay $10bn to settle 95,000 claims linking it to cases of non-Hodgkin's Lymphoma, like David's type of leukaemia. More than $1bn of that has been set aside for future claims.

While some countries and more than 40 of our own local councils have banned weedkillers containing RoundUp's key ingredient, glyphosate, RoundUp remains the most popular weedkiller in the UK and around the world.

We cannot at this stage conclusively say that any weedkiller was a factor in David's diagnosis. But keep that stuff the hell away from my family.

We had spent years trying to reduce our impact, remove our pollution, eliminate our toxins and now this – a disease that can lie undisturbed and inactive in the body for up to 15 years before symptoms present.

I'd love to be able to say that in the face of adversity we never wavered in our principles, but my first reaction was to take out the trash. I had deep cleaned the house, thinking that if I could make the place especially clear and simple and easy to live in, it would help take the pressure off as we dealt with whatever came next. But this was a couple of months into lockdown and with the much avoided recycling centre resolutely shut, a small cardboard box of accumulated broken glass became the focus of my frustration, anger and fear.

With our bin men and women understandably refusing to handle broken glass with the usual recycling collection and our household unable to do anything else with it for several more months, I could have left it in the corner of the kitchen but instead I dragged the black wheelie bin out from its dusty corner and dumped it in. I thought I'd feel guilty, but all I got was an overpowering sense of relief.

That was it, though. The otherwise empty bin was collected that week, replaced in its dusty corner and it hasn't re-emerged since.

Meanwhile, the other changes we had made became more important, not less. The plant-based diet, with its undeniable links to beneficial human health, became more important. Not spending money on stuff we didn't need made more sense. Knowing what was in the products we exposed ourselves to was crucial. Taking a breath and a step back became fundamental.

We all know that we need to look after the environment globally so we can all enjoy clean air, clean water and the like. But suddenly our efforts to look after the environment were looking a lot like our efforts to look after ourselves every day.

Reducing our impact, supporting regeneration and trying our damnedest to remove pollutants has taken on a new urgency with this reminder that we are of this world right down to the cells in our bodies. Its destruction destroys us – not vaguely or in some mystical tie-dyed crystal-waving way but clinically, starkly and absolutely.

The battle to 'save the world' is always being fought with a crucial psychological handicap, that we believe the problem is distant, geographically or in time. To the average consumer, even the dire warnings from experts always seem to refer to catastrophe in 50 or 100 years' time. We take that to mean we have time, that this isn't a threat for right now and certainly not for us. But it is hitting hard, right now, everywhere. We might not be able to see it, yet, but the way we treat our planet is already affecting us in the most real, personal, vital ways. Well, our household has just got that message loud and clear.

If you had told us that day in the back garden that stepping off a trampoline onto a beanbag would start a chain reaction that would make us change the way we thought about every part of what we do every day, I would have run a mile. We were and still are busy people trying to get by with two small kids and no spare time or headspace. We just didn't need the hassle.

But these changes have given us things we never anticipated, many of which have nothing to do with environmentalism. For us, taking a step back and re-evaluating everything has slotted together previously disparate, ill-fitting aspects of our lives. Life is now simpler, easier and cheaper.

And four years into the rest of our lives, maybe we, and the people around us are starting to be comfortable with the identity we now occupy. The people we have to be if we want to avoid greenwashing our own lives.

We know above all else that we need to keep working at all this, keep moving forward, keep pursuing that addictive sense of empowerment that comes from identifying a problem and changing it – the empowerment that comes, ultimately, from making our own decisions about how we live and why.

So half the family farm is now set to become one of the biggest broadleaf woodland creation projects in the region while the other half becomes an equally significant regenerative farming project.

Traditional fields that once contained a single crop are giving way to a different kind of agriculture – 'agroforestry' – where crops are grown and a mixture of animals raised between fruit and nut trees and the wide strips of undisturbed ground around and beneath them.

Going zero has not been a smooth process. It has been confusing, regularly imperfect, often hilarious, and occasionally bizarre. We make plenty of mistakes as we look for answers that sometimes aren't there. At least not yet.

This whole thing can't be an intense but short-lived activity. It's how it has to be, because this is the fight of and for our lives. As a species dependent on a global biosphere, economically and now suddenly very personally.

I wanted this book to be entertaining and upbeat, inclusive and positive. But I've also tried to be honest. And honestly, as we have dug into the data and delved into the detail, what we have found frightens me to my core, and not even simply for some distant day in our children's futures – for our present day because the future has already come to meet us.

Most of the natural world has been destroyed since 1970. The precise figure is 68%. A quarter of what's left is now threatened with extinction. Just 4% of all creatures on earth are wild. Everything else is either human or managed for our consumption.

But we're not wreaking this havoc because we're living it up. This is default destruction as a byproduct of everyday human existence. This is the result of seven billion people just trying to get by, most of whom aren't ever going to get on a plane or eat much meat anyway. The rest aren't all standing in ancient forests with chainsaws, or personally pitching plastic into the Atlantic. We're just going to work, doing the weekly shop, dealing with the pile of washing and a million other semi-automatic actions.

Those everyday actions amount to casual annihilation, and that's what scares me the most.

I have always been one of those people who hoped – assumed – that there would be a miraculous fix out there somewhere so we could remain reassured in our routines and cultural norms and societal parameters.

But normal isn't working. It hasn't ever worked and it won't ever work. We have run out of time to wait for as yet unknown tech to reveal a way out of this mess, or for the world's politicians to present a unified approach to fighting back.

To limit global warming to two degrees, carbon emissions should already be falling by 3% a year. The latest figures suggest the world is currently on course for a three degree temperature rise.

As I write, a new report from the UN suggests that national targets made so far will only deliver a 1% reduction in greenhouse gas emissions by 2030. It needs to be 45% to adhere to the Paris

Agreement. Only 75 of the 197 signatories of that agreement even submitted their targets in time to be assessed by the UN, and some of the biggest emitters such as the US, India and China still hadn't come up with a plan at the time of writing. It is such a pathetic, ambivalent non-response by those who promised to save the world it makes me want to scream.

António Guterres, secretary general of the United Nations, is clear that governments are nowhere close to the level of ambition needed to meet the goals of the Paris Agreement, describing the most recent round of data on climate change and emissions as 'code red for humanity':

'The evidence is irrefutable: greenhouse gas emissions are choking our planet & placing billions of people in danger. Global heating is affecting every region on Earth, with many of the changes becoming irreversible. We must act decisively now to avert a climate catastrophe.'

To save ourselves if nothing else, we now have no choice but to do this individually, directly, from the ground up. As activist Naomi Klein says far more eloquently than I can: 'There are no non-radical options left before us.'

Well bring on radical. From one entirely insignificant speck of humanity to another, let's snatch back control of our lives in every way we can think of and never let go, because there is still a tiny, beautiful chance that the future could still be bright indeed.

Between us, and against all the odds, I still believe we have the power to deliver such a future. It is now clear that we're the only ones that can.

Let's unleash that power. Now.

Top 10 Ways to Lower Your Impact

Going zero has been about a shift in underlying attitude, rather than trying to master a bewildering array of details. So here are the key principles we've adopted to try to make the change a little easier and less overwhelming.

1 Ask yourself the three questions: Are you comfortable about how this item or service has reached you? Are you comfortable with its environmental impact while you use it? Are you comfortable about what happens to it afterwards? Deciding the answers will, inevitably, lead to more questions about production processes and resource use sometimes, but hopefully they will help stop you falling down an information rabbit hole....

2 Try to think of the intrinsic value of everything that passes through your hands and work backwards from there. You will quickly find you automatically conserve and protect, and try to re-use it by default. That goes for physical items and transient resources like water and electricity as well as people's time and effort.

3 Everybody loves a mantra, especially when they all start with the same letter: Reuse, repair, rent, recycle....

4 ...reduce. The fastest way to have the biggest impact in every-day life, without exerting too much effort or burning up too many grey cells, is to cut consumption itself - from the amount of food on our plates to the number of purchases we make. Speaking of which....

5 ...slow down. Inject some space between you and your purchases, especially the discretionary ones. Jumping off the retail conveyor belt and taking time out to consider whether you really need that item or experience gives you back that all-important control – over your bank balance if nothing else. Don't fall for those sneaky selling signals or the artificial hype around certain events. Consumer group Which? says Black Friday is 99.5% BS.

6 Make it sustainable – in every sense. When you do need to buy, make sure it's built to last. When you make lifestyle changes, be confident you can see them through, allow them to bed in, become normal and something you no longer have to think too hard about.

7 Never assume that someone somewhere in the process has tak-en responsibility for the environmental impact of the product or service you use, especially when it is sitting on the brightly lit shelf of a well-known retailer. Especially when there's a picture of the world on them, a green tick or claims to be 'eco-friendly' with little to back it up. Take back control and make your own independent decisions. See tip 1!

8 Just because it is mainstream or established doesn't make some-thing the best approach. Christmas crackers are the perfect example. But do take lessons from history. We're at the end of a huge 60 year long social experiment that has destroyed our health, wealth and planet in its pursuit of new sources of revenue for the few. If you're looking for ways to make things cheaper, easier and more sustainable, you won't go too far wrong with a few tips from your gran.

9 Forget about trying to do this perfectly. It's impossible anyway. Just go for it. Start something now and give yourself permission to revisit and revise later. I'm pretty sure that's how evolution works anyway.

10 Be empowered. Be bold. We are already changing the future.

Acknowledgements

It turns out that writing a book is a really weird experience, especially when it's your first, it's about your own life and you're doing it in the middle of a global pandemic. Above all, though, it is an immense privilege so thank you Martin Hickman for asking me to do it in the first place, guiding me through the process and being so generous with your encouragement as well as your editing skills.

Second, and for what it's worth, my very best wishes to the independent climate and habitat experts out there. Please believe you're not shouting into a vacuum any longer.

Thank you to the band of proofreaders who kept me on the straight and narrow, especially when I went diving into papers produced by those experts. Dan Fish, sorry, Johnson, several current and former staff at the UK's Environment Agency, Amber Harris, Sarah Farrant, my mum Dr Annie Hughes who, along with my dad form the original empowerment couple.

Thanks to Lucie McInerney and particularly Linda Taylor (one of the great women of Fleet Street) at the *Independent* for letting a journalist whose patch had been finance and economics for 20 years fulfil her childhood dream. And for their encouragement, support and indulgence, particularly when I got completely over-excited about doing so.

Thank you Emma Kenny, who, in the process of being interviewed for an article about the psychology of Cop 26, will probably never know that she unwittingly managed to alleviate an eco anxiety cloud that struck at exactly the wrong time.

Thanks to the people who let us question everything about everything and then bang on about it for years – the entire Brewer clan comes particularly to mind!

Bruges – we will get there one day. And in the meantime, you lot are an awesome, generous and hilarious little band. The pornstar Martini girls and boys – you know who you are and why we'll always be in this together.

P&T. What incredible people you are. Pride doesn't start to cover it. Thank you for letting me duck out of bedtime and Sunday soup and bike rides more than once to get this done.

But above all others, David. I still have no idea why a rural traditionalist decided to marry a vegetarian townie but I count my lucky stars every day that you did. What an extraordinary thing to not simply re-evaluate everything from the ground up but to champion this journey in ways and at scales I could never have imagined.

You are the real pioneer in all this and I can't wait to get my hands in the soil, in the water, and above all to be at your side as we plant the first of those 100,000 trees with the kids. If we can, as we hope, change the future for our little corner of the world, it will be because of you. I've said so once before but it's worth stating again – you make this so much more than a 'little life'.

Sources of Information

Intergovernmental Panel on Climate Change
www.ipcc.ch/
The Nobel Peace Prize winning department of the UN that assesses scientific research around climate change.

United Nations Environment Programme
www.unep.org
The part of the global organisation responsible for coordinating responses to environmental issues within the United Nations system.

World Economic Forum
www.weforum.org
The international organisation for public-private cooperation. In other words, the place where business meets politics.

UK Environmental Audit Committee
www.parliament.uk/committee/62/environmental-audit-committee
The parliamentary committee which measures the impact of government and non-departmental public bodies.

Green Alliance
www.green-alliance.org.uk/
Charity and think tank focused on pushing leadership on environmental matters in the UK.

ShareAction
www.shareaction.org
Not for profit organisation that uses the investment system to push for beneficial change for savers, communities and the environment from a shareholder platform.

Make My Money Matter

makemymoneymatter.co.uk/

Campaign group driving transparency and responsibility in the world of pension investments.

Taskforce for Climate-related Financial Disclosures

www.fsb-tcfd.org/

Organisation pushing companies to disclose their carbon emissions.

Rainforest Alliance Network

www.ran.org

Campaign group working to protect forests, climate and human rights.

Greenpeace

www.greenpeace.org.uk

Global environmental NGO that needs little introduction.

Monga Bay

www.mongabay.com

A global environmental and conservation news platform populated by more than 800 specialist journalists around the world.

More Reading

- *Zero Waste Home*, Bea Johnston, Penguin Books, 2016
- *Seasonal Food: A Guide to What's in Season When and Why*, Paul Waddington, Eden Project Books, 2009.
- *Doughnut Economics*, Kate Raworth, Random House Business Books, 2017
- *There Is No Planet B: A Handbook for the Make or Break Years*, Mike Berners-Lee, Cambridge University Press, 2021
- *How to Live a Low-Carbon Life*, Chris Goodall, Earthscan/Routledge, 2007
- *The Uninhabitable Earth: A Story of the Future*, David Wallace-Wells, Crown Publishing Group, 2019
- *How Bad are Bananas?: The Carbon Footprint of Everything*, Mike Berners-Lee, 2nd Edition, Profile, 2020
- *Feral*, George Monbiot, Penguin Books, 2003
- *Wilding: The Return to Nature of a British Farm*, Isabella Tree, Pan Macmillan, 2019
- *This Changes Everything: Capitalism vs. Climate*, Naomi Klein, Penguin Books, 2015
- *Investing to Save the Planet*, Alice Ross, Penguin Books, 2020
- *A Life on Our Planet*, Sir David Attenborough, Ebury Publishing, 2020
- *Nobody is Too Small to Make a Difference*, Greta Thunberg, Penguin Books, 2019
- *The Dasgupta Review,* https://assets.publishing.service.gov.uk/government/uploads/system/uploads/attachment_data/file/957292/Dasgupta_Review_-_Abridged_Version.pdf

References

1. https://www.independent.co.uk/environment/mcdonalds-beef-burgers-amazon-rainforest-deforestation-cargill-bunge-a7741541.html

2. https://www.ncbi.nlm.nih.gov/pubmed/25813067

3. https://curia.europa.eu/jcms/upload/docs/application/pdf/2019-07/cp190092en.pdf

4. By 2019 the plastics industry was still fighting its corner. It hasn't worked. In response to an appeal by a plastics industry trade body that tried to block the official labelling of BPA as hazardous, the European Court of Justice upheld a ruling by the European Chemicals Agency that it was officially a 'substance of very high concern' or SVHC.

5. Yes, if you're wondering what on earth I was thinking, that pricey baby's bottle was indeed swept off the high chair tray within 24 hours – smashed into tiny, useless and quite hazardous bits. He didn't need it in the end and I never replaced it.

6. https://www.greenpeace.org.uk/news/supermarkets-more-plastic-than-ever/

7. Check the type of plastic the item is made from via the number in the 'chasing arrows' triangle first though as some are unsuitable for repeated use, such as number 1 PET plastic used for products including single-use bottled water.

8. Napper, I. E. & Thompson, R. C. (2019), Environmental Deterioration of Biodegradable, Oxo-biodegradable, Compostable, and Conventional Plastic Carrier Bags in the Sea, Soil, and Open-Air Over a 3-Year Period Environmental Science and Technology

9. http://www.wrap.org.uk/sites/files/wrap/Understanding%20plastic%20packaging%20FINAL.pdf

10. At the time of writing.

11. https://www.mcgill.ca/newsroom/channels/news/some-plastic-your-tea-300919

12. *How Bad Are Bananas*, M. Berners-Lee, Profile, 2020, p39.

13. I'm happy to have the cost of better food debate though, not least because our food spend as a nation has dropped from 25% of our household spend in the 1970s to only 17% today.

14. https://ora.ox.ac.uk/objects/uuid:b0b53649-5e93-4415-bf07-6b0b1227172f/download_file?file_format=pdf&safe_filename=Reducing_foods_environment_impacts_Science%2B360%2B6392%2B987%2B-%2B-Accepted%2BManuscript.pdf&type_of_work=Journal+article

15. https://www.ecocenter.org/toxic-any-speed-healthy-cars

16. https://www.epa.gov/indoor-air-quality-iaq/volatile-organic-compounds-impact-indoor-air-quality

17. that the kids instantly snatch away.

18. *How Bad Are Bananas*, Mike Berners-Lee, Profile, 2020, p 40.

19. https://www.water.org.uk/

20. Office for National Statistics

21. https://www.sciencedirect.com/science/article/abs/pii/S0269749117307686

22. https://www.sciencedirect.com/science/article/abs/pii/S2468584417300119

23. http://abe-research.illinois.edu/pubs/factsheets/styrofoam.pdf

24. https://www.frontiersin.org/articles/10.3389/fmars.2018.00071/full

25. https://marinesciences.uconn.edu/styrene/

26. More than 70 big US and several entire states rolled out a ban years ago, including New York and Washington, DC

27. https://www.pml.ac.uk/News_and_media/News/Are_we_underestimating_microplastics_in_the_marine

28. https://www.sciencedaily.com/releases/2018/02/180205125728.htm

29. https://www.nature.com/articles/s41598-017-10813-0

30. https://www.cell.com/current-biology/fulltext/S0960-9822(18)30086-1

31. https://www.sciencedirect.com/science/article/abs/pii/
S0048969718341159?_ga=2.250744134.1143759189.1614362058-7568624
62.1612382021&via%3Dihub

32. List sourced from WWF

33. *How Bad Are Bananas?*, Mike Berners-Lee, Profile, 2020, p32.

34. https://ourworldindata.org/land-use

35. https://ec.europa.eu/environment/archives/eussd/food.htm

36. https://www.cdc.gov/biomonitoring/Phthalates_FactSheet.html

37. https://www.sciencedirect.com/science/article/abs/pii/
S2468584417300119

38. https://www.nature.com/articles/s43017-020-0039-9

39. https://committees.parliament.uk/committee/62/environmental-au-
dit-committee/news/136508/online-giants-and-tech-powerhouses-in-eye-
of-the-storm-as-uk-battles-ewaste-tsunami/

40. https://www.ons.gov.uk/economy/environmentalaccounts/datasets/
materialconsumptionintheunitedkingdom2000to2013

41. https://www.weforum.org/agenda/2016/11/how-life-could-
change-2030/

42. https://www.pwc.com/hu/en/kiadvanyok/assets/pdf/sharing-econo-
my-en.pdf

43. https://www.statista.com/statistics/194424/amount-spent-on-toys-
per-child-by-country-since-2009/

44. https://www.bbc.co.uk/newsround/51451737

45. https://www.ucsusa.org/resources/ride-hailing-problem-climate

46. https://www.imo.org/en/MediaCentre/HotTopics/Pages/Reducing-greenhouse-gas-emissions-from-ships.aspx

47. https://www.epa.gov/ghgemissions/global-greenhouse-gas-emissions-data

48. Public experiences of and attitudes towards air travel: 2014 - GOV. UK (www.gov.uk)

49. C02 emissions from commercial aviation: 2013, 2018, and 2019, International Council on Clean Transportation (theicct.org)

50. Depending on the aircraft and number of passengers each is carrying, among other factors.

51. https://theicct.org/publications/C02-emissions-commercial-aviation-2020

52. https://climate.leeds.ac.uk/news/aviation-contributes-3-5-to-human-caused-climate-change/

53. https://climate.leeds.ac.uk/news/aviation-contributes-3-5-to-human-caused-climate-change/

54. Rail emissions | ORR Data Portal

55. *How Bad Are Bananas*, Mike Berners-Lee, Profile, 2020, p33.

56. http://emission.org.uk/for-hospitality/

57. https://www.ofgem.gov.uk/publications-and-updates/infographic-promoting-sustainable-energy-future

58. *How Bad Are Bananas*, Mike Berners-Lee, Profile. 2020, p29.

59. https://www.policyconnect.org.uk/cc/news/mps-call-green-heat-roadmap-2020-olympic-style-delivery-body-tackle-uks-27m-%E2%80%98uncomfortable-home

60. https://sw-consulting.co.uk/carbon-calculator

61. https://hbr.org/2016/10/the-behavioral-economics-of-recycling

62. https://www.researchgate.net/publication/303263301_The_Effect_of_Recycling_versus_Trashing_on_Consumption_Theory_and_Experimental_Evidence?amp%3BenrichSource=Y292ZXJQYWdlOzMwMzI2MzMwMTtBUzozNjI1MTA4NjQ2NjY2MjRAMTQ2MzQ0MDczMzYzOA%3D%3D&amp%3Bel=1_x_2

63. https://assets.publishing.service.gov.uk/government/uploads/system/uploads/attachment_data/file/918270/UK_Statistics_on_Waste_statistical_notice_March_2020_accessible_FINAL_updated_size_12.pdf

64. Unless we're talking about Pyrex or windows, which are manufactured a little differently.

65. https://www.britglass.org.uk/our-work/recycling

66. https://www.britglass.org.uk/sites/default/files/1709_0001-E1-17_Recycled%20content_0.pdf

67. https://www.britglass.org.uk/sites/default/files/1709_0001-E1-17_Recycled%20content_0.pdf

68. https://www.theguardian.com/business/2019/may/23/recycling-steel-could-give-lifeline-to-the-industry-report-says

69. *How Bad Are Bananas*, M. Berners-Lee, Profile, 2020 p49, p53, p77.

70. https://www.ed.ac.uk/files/atoms/files/pc-carbonfootprints-jh-ecci2.pdf

71. *How Bad Are Bananas*, M. Berners-Lee, Profile 2020, p43.

72. https://www.ofcom.org.uk/about-ofcom/latest/media/media-releases/2020/lockdown-leads-to-surge-in-tv-screen-time-and-streaming

73. https://www.sciencedirect.com/science/article/abs/pii/S0921344920307072?via%3Dihub

74. https://www.sciencedirect.com/science/article/abs/pii/S0921344920307072?via%3Dihub

75. https://www.purdue.edu/newsroom/releases/2021/Q1/turn-off-that-camera-during-virtual-meetings,-environmental-study-says.html

76. https://www.ovoenergy.com/ovo-newsroom/press-releases/2019/november/think-before-you-thank-if-every-brit-sent-one-less-thank-you-email-a-day-we-would-save-16433-tonnes-of-carbon-a-year-the-same-as-81152-flights-to-madrid.html

77. https://www.iea.org/reports/data-centres-and-data-transmission-networks

78. https://www.ran.org/bankingonclimatechange2020/

79. https://www2.deloitte.com/us/en/insights/industry/financial-services/esg-investing-performance.html

80. Net inflows according to Morningstar.

81. According to transaction network Calastone.

82. There are plenty of reasons that, as I write, the oil drilling contracts offered up by ex US President Donald Trump in the Arctic National Wildlife Refuge have been ignored by every big player out there. None of them include a deep concern for polar bears.

83. https://www.morningstar.co.uk/uk/news/209411/sustainable-funds-record-breaking-year.aspx

84. https://assets.publishing.service.gov.uk/government/uploads/system/uploads/attachment_data/file/957292/Dasgupta_Review_-_Abridged_Version.pdf

85. *How Bad Are Bananas*, M. Berners-Lee, Profile, 2020, p82.

86. http://esciencenews.com/articles/2011/07/28/growing.livestock.farm.linked.increased.risk.blood.cancers

87. https://globalewaste.org/

88. https://committees.parliament.uk/committee/62/environmental-audit-committee/news/136508/online-giants-and-tech-powerhouses-in-eye-of-the-storm-as-uk-battles-ewaste-tsunami/

89. https://www.who.int/teams/environment-climate-change-and-health/settings-populations/children/e-waste

90. https://www.bath.ac.uk/announcements/rise-of-eco-anxiety-affecting-more-and-more-children-says-bath-climate-psychologist/

91. https://www.statista.com/statistics/606684/world-production-of-lithium/#:~:text=Lithium%20mines%20produced%20an%20estimated,was%20just%2028%2C100%20metric%20tons

92. https://news.un.org/en/story/2020/06/1067272

93. IEA (2020), C02 Emissions from Fuel Combustion: Overview, IEA, Paris https://www.iea.org/reports/C02-emissions-from-fuel-combustion-overview

94. https://assets.publishing.service.gov.uk/government/uploads/system/uploads/attachment_data/file/918270/UK_Statistics_on_Waste_statistical_notice_March_2020_accessible_FINAL_updated_size_12.pdf

95. The drop is mostly due to lower rates of green recycling from things like garden cuttings since 2013, but you'd still hope we might be doing better on the recycling front with each year that passes.

96. https://www.thejakartapost.com/news/2020/05/10/ineffective-recycling-compounds-indonesias-marine-waste-problem.html

97. https://www.nao.org.uk/report/the-packaging-recycling-obligations/

98. https://www.nao.org.uk/report/the-packaging-recycling-obligations/

99. Waste and recycling management is a devolved matter.

100. https://assets.publishing.service.gov.uk/government/uploads/system/uploads/attachment_data/file/957292/Dasgupta_Review_-_Abridged_Version.pdf p24.

101. https://assets.publishing.service.gov.uk/government/uploads/system/uploads/attachment_data/file/957292/Dasgupta_Review_-_Abridged_Version.pdf p7

Kate Hughes is a national newspaper journalist and columnist. She is Money Editor for Independent.co.uk, for whom she also writes about sustainability. She is a commentator on BBC radio. She lives with her husband David and their two children in Somerset, England.

www.canburypress.com